THE UNIQUENESS AND UNIVERSALITY
OF JESUS CHRIST

THE UNIQUENESS AND UNIVERSALITY OF JESUS CHRIST

In Dialogue with the Religions

Edited by

MASSIMO SERRETTI

Translated by

Teresa Talavera *and*
David C. Schindler

WILLIAM B. EERDMANS PUBLISHING COMPANY
GRAND RAPIDS, MICHIGAN / CAMBRIDGE, U.K.

First published 2001 as
Unicità e universalità di Gesù Cristo: in dialogo con le religioni
a cura di Massimo Serretti
Edizioni San Paolo (Cinisello Balsamo [Milano])
ISBN 88-211-4423-0

Wm. B. Eerdmans Publishing Co.
255 Jefferson Ave. S.E., Grand Rapids, Michigan 49503 /
P.O. Box 163, Cambridge CB3 9PU U.K.

Printed in the United States of America

08 07 06 05 04   7 6 5 4 3 2 1

Library of Congress Cataloging-in-Publication Data

Unicità e universalità di Gesu Cristo. English.
     The uniqueness and universality of Jesus Christ: in dialogue with the religions /
edited by Massimo Serretti; translated by Teresa Talavera and David C. Schindler.
          p.   cm.
     Includes bibliographical references.
          ISBN 0-8028-2212-6 (pbk.: alk. paper)
     1. Theology of religions (Christian theology) 2. Jesus Christ — Person and offices.
     3. Catholic Church — Relations.   I. Serretti, Massimo.   II. Title.

BT83.85.U9513   2004
261.2 — dc22
                                                            2003068572

www.eerdmans.com

Contents

Contents

Preface

MASSIMO SERRETTI

The present volume gathers a number of studies on a contemporary philosophical and theological movement that goes by the name of the "pluralistic theology of religions." The studies, all based on a common working hypothesis, are the fruit of an International Research Project in Christology that brings together under the auspices of the Pontifical Lateran University (Rome, Italy) teachers and researchers from various schools and universities both in Italy and abroad.

The collection represents the results of a first phase of research whose primary aim has been to exhibit thematically the theoretical presuppositions of the pluralistic theology of religions. It thus highlights the premises, both acknowledged and unacknowledged, underlying these assumptions. Religion is a basic existential datum that has taken on various forms in different times and cultures; any account of it necessarily involves a general theory of religion and, undergirding that theory, an at least implicit theory of knowledge in general. The questions one might raise about the pluralistic theology of religions are of course numerous. The present volume focuses on the primary question of whether, and to what extent, the theories of knowledge on which this theology bases its account of religion and the religions are adequate. Even apart from differences in experience or religious affiliation, agreement and disagreement about these matters tend to be a function of the epistemological model that one presupposes. This is not to say, of course, that every religion can be explained by the prior assumption of some model of knowing. But certainly some such correspondence exists in the case of the theologies of the religions, which, after all, are so many intellectual efforts to say what religion is, what we ought to make of the plurality of religions, and what, if any, might be the relation among them.

The first part of our research, which we publish in the present volume, is thus particularly concerned with the question of *truth*. A theory of knowledge that admits the possibility of attaining to truth will yield one model of pluralism, while a theory that denies this possibility as a matter of principle will result in another conception of plurality altogether. Hence treating the question of truth from a general metaphysical point of view and consequently in matters of religion and religions, we establish at the same time the question of the quality of plurality. Thus we can justify a certain philosophical criticism, both epistemological and metaphysical, of the pluralistic theology of religions. This lays the foundation for an alternate model of coherence and of pluralism.

The discussion of truth and of the critique of truth claims intersects not only with issues surrounding epistemological realism, but also with the Judeo-Christian datum that the one true God has revealed himself, and that his self-revelation is a matter of historical fact. A certain ideology behind the main schools of the "pluralistic theology of religions," even before hitting Christianity, collides head-on with the very foundation of Jewish experience and identity as presented in the Old Testament. The cognitive relativism tries to update what is called "Lessing's axiom," that no particular, circumscribed historical fact can claim a general, transtemporal importance. But God's revelation on Sinai is a fact. The life of Jesus of Nazareth is also a fact. How seriously must we take the objection that the absolutization of these historical facts that occurred in a clearly defined time and place contradicts their status as universal religious phenomena, whose nature is supposedly defined by cultural particularity?

In order to get clear about this question, the first part of our work focuses on the link between the nature of truth, on the one hand, and the uniqueness and universality of Jesus Christ on the other. Does the claim that Jesus Christ is both unique and universal in fact necessarily lead to potential violence against other religions? Is the Christian truth claim truly an endless source of conflict with other religious traditions? Is there not built into the nature of Christian truth any inclination for openness to, and peaceful encounter with, other religions already? And even more radically, might not Christianity possess the key that will open the closed door of the historical datum of the plurality of religious ways?

Methodologically speaking, the studies gathered here follow a double track: they both critique the pluralist ideology and lay out a doctrine of truth and of the uniqueness and universality of Jesus Christ. Some of the studies sound a more critical note, attempting mainly to offer a balanced judgment of the assumptions underlying the religious and epistemological relativism or, as the case may be, the reductionism of ethical traits and that which is proper to a philosophy of culture and of cultures, that informs the pluralistic theologies of religions. One of the merits of this sort of critique is that it clarifies and unmasks ideologies that are widespread in society and models of thought that are influential in other domains of inquiry. Thanks to such pseudo-evidences that increasingly permeate Western societies, the pluralistic theologies of religions find an easy path lying before them.

This critical assessment is corroborated by another set of considerations that are more independent of present controversy and constructive in nature. The mystery of God communicated in the history of revelation, and definitively so in the economic order through Jesus Christ, has an identity and existence of its own. Revelation imparts a similar independence to man's knowledge of it. There is no need for a dialectical logic either to initiate or to deepen reflection on being, the true, the good, and the beautiful. Such reflection stands on its own. The same is true, analogously, for reflection on the mystery of God. This independence is the hidden root of the philosophical and theological creativity displayed in the studies collected in this volume. It is also a source of numerous insights that suggest ways to continue the research, as the team of authors is already doing. The results of this further research will appear in due course in a follow-up volume.

The studies presented here were conceived and written before the publication of *Dominus Jesus,* the Congregation for the Doctrine of the Faith's declaration on the unique and universal saving role of both Jesus Christ and his church. At the press conference prior to the promulgation of *Dominus Jesus,* Cardinal Ratzinger had this to say about the document:

> [It] flags some of the philosophical and theological assumptions under-
> lying today's widespread theologies of pluralism — which, of course, are
> different in many respects. I refer to the belief in the total impossibility
> of grasping or expressing the truth about God; a relativistic approach to

truth that holds that what is true for some may not be for others; a radical opposition between the logical Western mind and the symbolic Eastern mind; an exaggerated subjectivism that goes so far as to see reason as the sole source of knowledge; the emptying of the Incarnation of any metaphysical depth; the eclecticism of theologians who borrow categories from other religions without attending either to their internal consistency or to their incomparability with Christian faith; finally, the tendency to wrench the interpretation of Scriptural texts from the Church's Tradition and Magisterium.

Cardinal Ratzinger also notes that these assumptions lead some to "consider" "as a kind of fundamentalism that attacks the modern spirit and threatens tolerance and freedom" the very conviction that "there is a universal, binding, and valid truth in history itself, that this truth comes to pass in the person of Jesus Christ, and that it is transmitted by the Church's faith." But this very judgment makes the pluralists fiercely intolerant, so much so, in fact, that observers have recently begun to speak of the "intolerance of relativism." The cardinal himself highlights the loss that the uncritical assumption of the presuppositions he critiques inevitably brings:

> This principle of tolerance and respect for freedom is being manipulated and unduly exaggerated today. We see this when the principle is extended to matters of content, as if all the contents of all religions, indeed, even of non-religious worldviews, were somehow on the same footing, as if there were no longer any universal and objective truth, because God or the Absolute reveals itself under innumerable names — all of which are true. This false idea of tolerance goes together with the loss, the renunciation of the question of truth, which many today in fact judge to be irrelevant, or at best secondary. The intellectual weakness of contemporary culture is thus exposed: in the absence of the question of truth, the essence of religion can no longer be differentiated from its non-essence, faith from superstition, experience from illusion. In the end, if there is no serious claim to truth, it also becomes meaningless and contradictory to esteem the other religions, for there is no criterion for ascertaining what is positive in a given religion by distinguishing it from what is negative, or superstitious, or deceitful.

John Paul II offered an important interpretation of *Dominus Jesus,* whose intent was to clarify not so as to halt or slow down interreligious dialogue but to foster it in truth, in his Angelus of 1 October 2000: "Our confession that Christ is the only Son through whom we ourselves see the face of the Father (cf. Joh 14:8), is not an arrogance that holds the other religions in contempt." "The document clarifies the essential points of Christian teaching. These do not hinder dialogue, but exhibit its foundations. For a dialogue without foundations would be doomed to degenerate into empty chatter." The document is meant "to clarify and, at the same time, to open."

It is in this spirit of openness that we offer this study to our readers, aware that only the truth, which is greater than the human mind (as Augustine says), can truly open man beyond himself.

Freedom, Truth, and Salvation

ANGELO CARDINAL SCOLA

In a recent discourse John Paul II set forth a clear vision of the organically structured body of disciplines to be cultivated by the Catholic university. Among these, of course, is theology, which, the Holy Father insisted, must strive to present the mystery of God "in the 'language' of the current generation."[1]

Now a significant feature of the "current generation" is the multiethnic, multicultural, and multireligious environment in which it finds itself. In this situation the truth claim of the Christian message — Jesus "is the stone which was rejected by you, the builders, but which has become the head of the corner. And there is salvation in no one else, for there is no name under Heaven among men by which we must be saved" (Acts 4:11-12) — takes on its full dramatic significance.

The magisterium of the church, particularly since the Second Vatican Council, has willingly taken up the challenge posed by the plurality of religions; it has come to see ever more clearly that its relationship with the religions of the world is an "intrinsic necessity for the faith."[2] And in the recent postsynodal exhortation *Ecclesia in Asia,* John Paul II affirms that "from the Christian point of view, interreligious dialogue is much more

---

1. John Paul II, "Inaugurazione dell'Anno Accademico della Pontificia Università Lateranense (16 novembre 1999)," *L'Osservatore Romano,* 17 November 1999, 5.

2. J. Ratzinger, *Il nuovo popolo di Dio* (Brescia, 1971), 391-92.

than a way of promoting mutual familiarity with, and enrichment by, other faiths; it is part of the Church's mission to evangelize, an expression of her mission ad gentes."[3]

The affirmation that interreligious dialogue is intrinsically necessary for faith, and even more, the conviction that such dialogue is an expression of the mission of the church, is hardly obvious today. On the contrary, it is often seen as problematic, not only by representatives of non-Christian religions but even by many Christians.

It is incumbent upon theology to study this controverted affirmation more deeply, according to the laws of the *intellectus fidei,* and to show its inner coherence. Such is the aim of the Research Project on Christology instituted at Lateran University two years ago under the direction of Professor Marcello Bordoni, whose first results appear in the present volume.

The acknowledgment that interreligious dialogue is intrinsically necessary for the church's mission *ad gentes* requires the development of a *theology of religions* that situates the religions within the one trinitarian plan of salvation, with full respect for all parties. In fact, there is already a certain standard typology of approaches to the question that subdivides them into *exclusivist, inclusivist,* and *pluralist* models, respectively (needless to say, there is great variety within each model).[4]

While the exclusivist model lapses into a dualistic account of God's plan of salvation and revelation, the pluralist position fails to do justice to the integrity of the Christian faith. Above all, it misses the heart of religion on account of its failure to grasp the link between religion and truth. The result of this failure is an incapacity to give interreligious dialogue a suitable foundation. Finally, the inclusivist position, which seems at first glance to be the most respectful of revelation among the three,[5] nonetheless risks a certain narrow-mindedness insofar as an underlying conceptualist approach to theology tends to prevent it from overcoming the extrinsicism between faith and reason, revelation and religion.

I have elsewhere argued that the notion of truth as *event* provides the adequate foundation for the theology of religions,[6] which can best be de-

---

3. John Paul II, *Ecclesia in Asia,* 31.

4. See A. Amato, "Cristologia e religioni non cristiane. Problematica e attualità: considerazioni introduttive," *Rassegna di Teologia* 1 (1990): 143-68.

5. See Commissio Theologica Internationalis, *Christianismus et religiones* (30 September 1996), in *Enchiridion Vaticanum* 15 (1996): 986-1113.

6. See A. Scola, *Questioni di Antropologia Teologica* (Rome, 1997), 155-73.

veloped within reflection on what I call the "original structure." This reflection could be termed an *ontological anthropology*. Combining core insights of phenomenology and transcendental thought, we can elaborate a symbolic ontology capable of resisting any slide into relativism. This approach, which unites absoluteness and historicity, necessity and freedom, furnishes the key to the original and unitary link between revelation and human freedom — and therefore, to the unity between revelation and salvation: "The historical nature of the truth as event reveals that it is nothing other than the realization of the salvation addressed to man's freedom. Truth, occurring as event, saves those who welcome it."[7] I would suggest that it is within this framework that the terms discussed in this volume — "freedom," "truth," and "salvation" — can be adequately dealt with.

Nevertheless, even on the supposition — which is only that — of its validity, the approach I am proposing is only a first step. It is not enough to reflect on revealed truth in terms of *event*. We must also demonstrate that revelation coincides with the singular *event* of the human history of the Son of God: Jesus Christ dead and risen — and that the absoluteness of this fact not only takes away nothing from the religions but actually sets their distinctive truth claims in relief.

The postsynodal exhortation *Ecclesia in Asia* offers some helpful indications on how to proceed:

> from the beginning to the end of time, Jesus is the only universal Mediator. Christ is the source of saving grace through the communication of the Holy Spirit even for those who do not explicitly profess faith in him. We believe that Jesus Christ, true God and true man, is the only Savior, since He alone — the Son — has brought to completion the universal plan of salvation. As the definitive manifestation of the mystery of the Father's love towards all people, Jesus is in fact unique and "it is this unique singularity of Christ that confers upon him an absolute and universal significance, and so, while he is in history, he is the center and the end of this same history" (see *Redemptor Hominis*, 6). No person, no nation, no culture is impervious to the call of Jesus, who speaks to the heart of the human condition itself.[8]

7. Scola, 166.
8. John Paul II, *Ecclesia in Asia*, 14.

Drawing on this citation, I would like to suggest three themes that in my opinion are central. I will limit myself to the briefest sketch.

The first refers to the couplet "unique-universal" that figures in the title of the present volume. This pair of terms obviously has to do with the uniqueness of Jesus Christ as the mediator of salvation. But this uniqueness has to do with eschatological resurrection. Does or does not the resurrection of the flesh have any significance for God? Someone has used the image of the grain of sand which, despite its impurity, remains encased in the pearl. We face, on a more radical level, the question of the indispensable role of freedom's "response" to the gift of the Trinity's self-revelation in Jesus Christ. This question goes to the core of the theology of the religions.

Second, it is important to highlight the document's reference to the Holy Spirit. It seems to me particularly important to bear in mind the double track that the passage cited from *Ecclesia in Asia* suggests to us. On the one hand we need to become more aware of the role of the Spirit of the risen Christ in universalizing the work of salvation ("Christ is the source of saving grace through the communication of the Holy Spirit"); on the other hand there is a link to be made between the work of the Spirit and the contemporaneity of Jesus' call to the freedom of each man, who lives in the dual unity of individual-community (the context in which the "religions" are situated) ("No person, no nation, no culture is impervious to the call of Jesus, who speaks from the heart of the human condition itself"). This second set of issues would be the place for reflection on the sacramental logic at the heart of Christian revelation.

Finally, if we take our bearings from the New Testament, we must zero in on what in my opinion is the core of a theological reflection on the eschatological and pneumatological character of the event of Jesus of Nazareth: a renewed deepening of soteriology. Jesus Christ is the one universal mediator because he is the definitive priest who pours out his Spirit from the cross, the maximal revelation of the Father's love.

It is in the tension between the cross and the resurrection that the perfect correspondence (analogy) between the trinitarian foundation and human freedom is achieved. This tension thus seems to provide the best way to approach interreligious dialogue and the task of elaborating a theology of religions. In the end the Christian's way cannot be any other than that of his Lord: the total giving of self.

It is hard to imagine a better testimony to this truth than the martyrdom of the monks of Tibirhine. Theologians would benefit greatly from pondering the testament of Fr. Christian de Chergé, prior of the monastery, who, before the tragic and glorious event, had in a certain sense worked out a profound, and perhaps peerless, *intellectus fidei* of what would happen:

> If one day I should become the victim of the terrorism that threatens every foreigner living in Algeria (and it might happen today), I would like for my community, my Church, my family to remember that my life was given to God and to that Country. I would like them to accept that the sole Master of every life cannot be alienated from this brutal death. . . . Evidently, my death will seem to prove right those who have rashly considered me a naïve or idealistic person: "Now tell us what you think!" But these people should know that my most piercing curiosity will finally be satisfied. This death is what may, if God wills, immerse my gaze in that of the father, to contemplate with him his children of Islam as he sees them, totally illuminated by the glory of Christ, the fruit of his Passion, clothed with the gift of the Spirit, whose secret joy will always be to establish communion, to reestablish likeness, playing with differences.[9]

9. *Osservatore Romano,* 8 June 1996.

The Uniqueness and Universality of Jesus Christ

WALTER CARDINAL KASPER

The Complex Situation of a World on the Way to Unity

The world's present situation is marked by two opposing characteristics. On the one hand we are faced with the phenomenon of globalization. The world has become, as it were, a "global village." Not only do financial currents travel electronically around the world millions of times each day, but modern means of communication give us access to information on a worldwide scale. Modern means of transport carry people and goods from one end of the world to the other in just a few hours.

Unfortunately, this has not made the world any more peaceful. Globalization creates new forms of dependence and injustice and gives the strong and the powerful new opportunities for domination. In fact, the confluence of peoples of different cultures gives rise to deep anxieties, which cause problems leading to hatred and rebellion. There is thus an expansion of particular interests and of ethnic and cultural conflicts. Some commentators speak of a coming "clash of civilizations" (Huntington), and in many places such a clash is already taking place amidst bloodshed. We need think only of Northern Ireland, Rwanda, Sudan, Bosnia, and Kosovo.

In the so-called developed societies there is an increasing disappearance of common values and basic convictions. Pluralism has enjoyed a downright explosive growth in every sphere of life and thought in our century. We notice an ever greater differentiation of ways of life, types of thought, orientations, worldviews, and styles of action. We have even reached the point where some question the validity of universal human rights common to all peoples and cultures; this is happening not only in authoritarian states such as China, but also among Western intellectuals. These thinkers consider the claim to universal human rights to be a neocolonialistic, Eurocentric mode of thinking.

This pluralism also affects the personal identity of the individual. Most people are obliged to live in a number of different worlds at once. The worlds of family, of work, of free time, of the private and the public, of economics and politics and culture are often isolated from one another. The result is a "patchwork identity," a syncretistic tapestry of interchangeable pieces drawn from the most disparate religious and cultural traditions. In this patchwork certain things are identified without concern for conceptual clarification and all the seams and fractures are left open.

The attempt to pick out from this dizzyingly vast multiplicity a thread that could unify and hold it together seems to be more and more hopeless. Postmodern philosophy has drawn certain conclusions from this situation. It consciously abandons the postulate of unity that until now has shaped Western thought as a whole. It advocates not only acceptance and tolerance of plurality, but a fundamental option in favor of pluralism. Postmodern thought has thus arrived at a new quantitative pluralism in which there are no longer any absolute values and norms. Reason has become plural in itself. Truth, humanity, and justice exist only in the plural. By the same token there is no longer one universally and definitively valid religion.

The Pluralism of Religions: A Challenge to Theology

Even if the world has always been pluralistic, we experience this pluralism in a new way today; we are becoming more conscious of it than ever before and we can no longer avoid the question of how to deal with it. This is a situation that calls Christianity fundamentally into question and that challenges the church in an entirely new way. The Second Vatican Council defined the Catholic Church precisely as a sign and instrument of unity and peace (*Lumen Gentium* [hereafter *LG*], 1, etc.). The church thus finds itself particularly challenged by the situation of the world today.

7

From the beginning, the church appeared on the scene with a double message. It has always resolutely maintained that every man, regardless of the color of his skin or his ethnic and cultural identity, is made in the image of God (Gen. 1:27), and that every individual possesses an unconditional dignity unique to him alone. Fundamental human rights therefore are valid both universally and for every individual personally. Since Vatican II, and especially under the present pontificate, the Catholic Church has been more committed than ever to universal respect for human rights.

This universalism is especially true for the church's salvific mission. Jesus sent out his disciples into the entire world, to all peoples, and to all men (Matt. 28:19; Mark 16:15; Luke 24:47; Acts 1:8). The mission of the church is therefore universal, and the church is missionary by its very essence (*Ad Gentes* [hereafter *AG*], 2). The church is not bound to a specific people, culture, language, or political or economic system. The church is, as it were, the oldest "global player." With Vatican II the church has come to understand itself as the universal sacrament of salvation and as a sign and instrument of unity (*LG*, 1, 9, 48; *Gaudium et Spes* [hereafter *GS*], 42, 45; *AG*, 1, 5, etc.). It transcends all ethnic, national, and cultural differences in the wish to unite all peoples, languages, and cultures in praise of the one God.

The designation of the one God as Father of all men suggests a second essential element of the Christian message. Alongside universality is the unity, indeed, uniqueness, of the church's message. The church preaches the one and only God (Deut. 6:4; Mark 12:29), who is the Father of all men, both good and evil (Matt. 5:45). It confesses the one Lord Jesus Christ (1 Cor. 8:6; Eph. 4:5). In no other name is there salvation (Acts 4:12). He is the only mediator between God and men (1 Tim. 2:5). He is the High Priest who has redeemed us once and for all (Heb. 7:27). This message has been transmitted to us once and for all (Jude 3).

It follows that there can be only one true church, the "one, holy, catholic, and apostolic church" that we profess in the creed. This church, according to the Catholic understanding, is united in the one common profession of faith in the only Lord Jesus Christ; in the celebration of the same sacraments, especially of the Eucharist as a sacrament of unity; and in one ministry of unity in the college of bishops with and under the successor of Peter (*LG*, 13).

Given the strong emphasis on the unity and uniqueness of Jesus Christ and of his church on the one hand, and the pluralistic situation of the modern and postmodern world on the other, it is not surprising that precisely this question of the unity and uniqueness of Jesus Christ should have aroused a broad, fierce debate both inside and outside of theology. In fact, not only has cultural pluralism increased, but the pluralism of religions is also becoming more and more clearly evident than in the past.

We are more aware today than in the past of the many centuries and millennia that preceded the coming of Jesus Christ into the world and of the many millions of people who, two thousand years after the birth of Christ, have not yet been seized by the Christian message and who live outside of Christianity. Is it possible that all these people will be lost for eternity? If so, how is this eternal loss compatible with the justice and mercy of God and with his desire to save all human beings?

Awareness of this multiplicity of religions is obviously nothing new. What is new, however, is the fact that globalization has brought this phenomenon home to us with unprecedented urgency. The religions, too, have grown closer in the world's "global village." They are no longer hermetically sealed from one another. They often coexist, indeed, overlap in one and the same country or city. Almost all of us live among people who belong to other religions, and whom we still esteem as human beings.

In our global situation tolerance, reciprocal respect, and peace among religions are a key to peace in the world as well as among and within peoples.

The Hypothesis of Religious Pluralism

This is the context in which the most recent theories of religious pluralism should be understood. Representatives of these newer approaches would include Raimundo Panikkar, John Hick, and Paul F. Knitter.

The question as such is not new. We find it already in Enlightenment figures such as Lessing as well as among exponents of liberal theology, especially Troeltsch, who accorded a maximum, but not absolute, validity to Christianity. The idealists, Hegel first among them, revolted against the Enlightenment's relativization of Christianity; it was Hegel who introduced the still current idea of the absoluteness of Christianity. Idealism is often blamed today for the totalitarian ideologies of the twentieth century. Following upon the collapse of these ideologies, it has come under attack as Eurocentric, imperialistic, and itself totalitarian; it is reproached for ig-noring the ineliminable multiplicity of reality and of cultures.

The pluralistic theory of religions arose within this context. Under-lying the pluralist theory is not merely the observation that there are many religions, but also the claim that there are many revelations and therefore many paths to, and mediators of, salvation. The pluralist account thus poses the sharpest problem when it comes to the unity of Jesus Christ and, more precisely, to the question of his role as the one universal mediator of salvation. This question obviously affects a central and fundamental point of Christian faith, one that pertains to the identity of Christianity and of the church.

In order to ground the pluralistic theories philosophically, various theologians have opted for a new theory of knowledge that appeals to Kantian epistemology. According to Kant, knowledge has access only to the "phenomenon," not to the "noumenon." This means that we know only what things are for us, not what they truly are in themselves. More recently, postmodern philosophy has replaced logic with aesthetics as the decisive criterion of truth. Indeed, there is even talk of a revival of myth.

Thus we know only what God means for us. We cannot grasp the es-sence of God in himself. Therefore it is impossible to ask about the objec-tive truth content of the many images and representations of God. Now if absolute being cannot be present in history, if there can be only ideal rep-resentations, concepts, images, or figures of the divine that point us toward transcendent reality, but never the appearance of that reality itself, then Christianity has no grounds for claiming absoluteness. Hick accordingly denies the identification of God with a single historical figure, with Jesus of Nazareth, an identification that he brands as mythological. Jesus Christ is relativized and equated with a religious genius who helps us discover that we are all children of God.

The fact that the pluralistic theology of religions assumes the funda-mental equivalence of all religions does not mean that its proponents re-gard all religions as equally valid, as if the differences between them were of no account. They are very far from such a superficial relativism. As a matter of fact, they insist that the religions harbor not only great and deep intuitions, but also destructive elements such as superstition and inhuman cruelty.

But the pluralists adopt an ethical and practical, rather than a theoret-ical, criterion for distinguishing among religions and assessing their value.

Religions are evaluated primarily in terms of their respective capacity to integrate man and the different spheres of life in a process that leads from "self-centeredness" to "reality-centeredness." The religion that most corresponds to, and promotes, the dignity of man therefore deserves special preference.

The question is whether this ultimately humanistic ethical and practical criterion is sufficient from a philosophical and theological point of view. It is indeed obvious that this criterion can justify both the primacy and the preferred status of one religion. But it cannot justify the singularity and uniqueness of a given religion, concretely of Christianity. This criterion can justify, at best, a supreme validity, but not an absolute one. We thus remain at a fundamental pluralism and dispute among religions.

We can take the argument even further and ask ourselves whether there can ever be an ethical criterion that does not necessarily presuppose a theoretical one. Who is to say what it is to be truly human? Might it not be that every ethical and practical criterion necessarily calls upon a theoretical judgment in order to answer this question? In fact, one's judgment will differ according to the image of man one assumes either consciously or unconsciously. Putting it radically, the question concerning the truth of reality cannot be evaded.

If the question concerning the truth is no longer asked, we are left with a purely aesthetic understanding of the world in which things are judged according to their subjective experiential content and where one eclectically chooses what seems to correspond best to one's own sensibility and concept of happiness. Self-service à la carte at the supermarket of religions is the order of the day, and contradictory affirmations are allowed to stand side by side without resolution. Faith in plurality and tolerance thus threatens to invert into indifference and apathy. It is no accident that postmodern thought leads, in a whole host of its spokesmen, to a nihilism whose forefather and archetype is Nietzsche.

The Doctrine of the Second Vatican Council

The unclarified presuppositions, the consequences, and not least the contradictions with the central and fundamental statements of sacred Scripture and tradition that we find in the pluralist account compel us to examine the theological tradition that was articulated above all by the Second

Vatican Council. In fact, already before this account arrived on the scene, Vatican II had dealt with the new approach to the problem on the basis of the church's own tradition. This serves as the basis for a whole host of Catholic approaches.

Vatican II overcame the previously widespread opinion that non-Christian religions contain only error and superstition. In its declaration on the church's relations with non-Christian religions, *Nostra Aetate,* the council stated plainly and clearly that the church does not deny any of "what in these religions is true and holy. She looks with respect upon those forms of action and of life, those precepts and doctrines that, although in many points different from what she herself believes and proposes, still not uncommonly reflect a ray of the truth that enlightens all men" (2). In its decree on the church's missionary activity, *Ad Gentes,* the council retrieved the doctrine of many fathers of the church and spoke of the truth and the grace (9), of the seeds of the Word (11), that can be found among the pagans thanks to a kind of hidden divine presence.

The council confirmed the theological doctrine according to which God, who is the salvation of all men (1 Tim. 2:4), contrives paths to salvation for those who through no fault of their own do not know Jesus Christ but try to act according to the divine will as made to known to them in the call of conscience under the influence of grace (*LG,* 16; cf. *GS,* 22).

Moreover, the council, in its declaration on religious freedom, *Dignitatis Humanae* (hereafter *DH*), while teaching clearly that the "one true religion" is "realized in the Catholic, apostolic Church," also taught that the duty to follow the truth touches and binds men "in their conscience"; since "the truth makes no claims except in virtue of the truth itself" (1, 3). The council thus appealed to the most ancient tradition in order to distance itself from certain missionary approaches; it rejected every form of constraint and pressure to join the Christian faith or, indeed, any religion. In fact, the act of faith is by nature a free act (*DH,* 10). The council thus recognized every man's right not only to adhere internally and privately to his religion, but also to profess it publicly.

The council's teaching is based on the witness of the New Testament. The letter to the Colossians and the prologue to John's Gospel in particular insist that everything was made in, through, and for Jesus Christ (Col. 1:15-16). Everything has been created through the Word who became man in Jesus Christ; he is the life and the light that enlightens every man (John 1:3-5, 9). This New Testament doctrine was developed by certain early fathers of the church who held that every reality, even the non-Christian religions, contains fragments *(logoi spermatikoi)* of the truth that fully appeared once and for all in Jesus Christ.

The encyclical *Redemptoris Missio*, on "the permanent validity of the missionary task" (1990), added a further important consideration to the teaching of the council. The encyclical argues not only christologically but also pneumatologically. The Spirit of God embraces everything, is present and active without any limitation in space or time. He works in the heart of every man who aspires to truth and goodness and who sincerely seeks God. The Spirit gives to each man light and strength to respond to his supreme vocation and offers to all the possibility "of coming in contact with the Paschal mystery in a way that only God knows." The Spirit is therefore at the origin of the existence and the question of every man's faith, a question that arises not only in specific situations but also because of the structure of his very existence. The presence and action of the Spirit concerns not only the individual man, "but also society and history, peoples, cultures, religions" (28).

Whether or not one should speak (with Rahner) of anonymous Christians in this context is another matter. The decisive point for us is simply that the Spirit of God can be present outside the visible church — both visibly and hiddenly.

The conciliar and postconciliar magisterium has thus laid the foundation for dialogue and cooperation with believers of other religions. Indeed, it has expressly fostered such dialogue. Popes Paul VI and John Paul II responded to this invitation to promote interreligious dialogue. Paul VI's reform of the curia established within this body an authority whose specific area of competence is interreligious dialogue.

The teaching of the council rendered obsolete the older exclusivist theory and praxis that reasoned that since Jesus Christ is the only mediator of salvation, no one can be saved if he does not profess the faith and belong to the church. *Extra ecclesiam nulla salus* was the famous axiom coined by Cyprian of Carthage (undoubtedly in the context of an intraecclesial dispute). Thanks to Augustine's disciple Fulgentius of Ruspe, this axiom later became a staple of the theological tradition; it was given special prominence at the Fourth Lateran Council.

The axiom was often interpreted to mean that all who do not know and profess the Christian faith are lost for eternity. This idea is hard for most people to understand today; it does not seem compatible with the justice and mercy of God, his desire for the salvation of all, and with solidarity among men.

Even before the council, but especially after it, the exclusivist theory was largely replaced in Catholic theology by an inclusivist alternative, albeit with variations on points of detail. This theory attempts, on the basis of the testimony of Scripture and of the church fathers, to conceive the salvation brought about once for all in Jesus Christ in a universal fashion that would include all that is true and good in other religions. On this view the salvation in which non-Christians can share if they live according to their consciences is not a salvation outside of Jesus Christ, but rather a salvation in and through him. This account has in the meantime become more or less the *opinio communis* of Catholic theology.

Unity in Multiplicity: The Christological and Trinitarian Perspective

More recent theories question the adequacy of the inclusivist account. Does it, they ask, do justice to the otherness of non-Christian religions? Or does it co-opt and absorb them? Does it not perhaps make them, contrarily to their own self-understanding, anonymously Christian? Is not this approach a camouflaged imperialism?

To deal with this question we need to rethink more deeply the question of the unity and uniqueness of Jesus Christ among the religions against the background of the trinitarian and christological profession of faith as a whole. This will lead us to a kenotic account of the problem of unity and multiplicity.

Let us begin by dwelling on the significance of faith in the unity and uniqueness of God. This faith unites Judaism, Christianity, and Islam, while distinguishing these three monotheistic religions from all others. Of course, it has a specific meaning in Christianity.

On the Christian understanding, faith in the one and only God cannot be understood in a merely quantitative sense: it means more than that "there is" only one God and not rather, say, two or three. The Bible affirms the unity of God not only in a quantitative sense, but, above all, in a qualitative and essential sense. The profession of faith in the one and only God stands against the background of the demand for a radical and comprehensive decision to adhere to God with one's whole heart, soul, and mind

(Mark 12:30 and par.). It is indeed impossible to serve two masters (Matt. 6:24). God is such that he takes us, absorbs us, and fills us in every fiber of our existence.

The theological tradition has deepened this idea speculatively. It has shown that by essence God is the reality that embraces and surpasses everything. Therefore, by essence God can be only one. Anyone who professes more than one God has not understood what the word "God" really means. Tertullian expressed this point in the formula: If God is not one God, he is no God.

The profession of faith in the one God includes belief that the one God is the God of all men who embraces everything and everyone. While polytheism posits a multiplicity of realities, peoples, and cultures, the profession of faith in the one God offers the sharpest possible contradiction to the fragmentation of reality and the clearest possible affirmation of the unity of the world and of mankind. The profession of faith in the one God says all men are brothers and sisters because they belong to one family under the one God who is in heaven. Thus the universal claim of the one God also preserves the ineliminable and inalienable value of the singular.

The deepest reason why the profession of faith in the one God does not eliminate but, on the contrary, includes multiplicity is the trinitarian confession of one God in three persons. This profession is the exegesis of the biblical claim that "God is love" (1 John 4:8, 16). The one God is not a solitary God, but rather from eternity is love who gives himself without measure, love in which the Father communicates to the Son and Father and Son are in communion in the Holy Spirit. Each one of the three persons is entirely God, entirely infinite, and each gives space to the others, communicating himself and, in this way, expropriating himself. In this kenotic form God is unity in multiplicity.

Since God is eternally love between Father, Son, and Spirit, a love that gives itself and strips itself, he can communicate himself entirely in Christ without renouncing or losing himself. The divinity of Jesus is shown in the stripping of himself (Phil. 2:6). The omnipotence of love does not need to impose itself, but can instead give and distribute itself, and it is precisely in this giving of self that it is itself. Such stripping of self is true and authentic only insofar as the divinity of the eternal Logos does not absorb and swallow his humanity, but rather accepts it in its specificity and liberates it into its distinctive being. Thus, as the church professes, in Jesus Christ divinity and humanity are neither mixed nor separated (*DS*, 302). Jesus Christ is unity in distinction and distinction in unity.

Thus the fact that the one God has once only, yet wholly, definitively, and unreservedly communicated himself historically in Jesus Christ is a basic conviction of the fathers of the church reflected in the church's ancient tradition. In him resides the fullness of divinity (Col. 1:19; 2:9). The historical coming of Jesus Christ has thus inaugurated the fullness of time (Mark 1:15; Gal. 4:4). This coming of the fullness of time is the accomplishment of the eternal mystery of God (Rom. 16:25; Eph. 1:9; Col. 1:26).

It follows necessarily from this that if God communicated himself entirely, definitively, and unreservedly in the concrete person and history of Jesus Christ, then Christ is the *id quo maius cogitari nequit,* that than which nothing greater can be thought (Anselm). He is also the *id quo Deus maius operari nequit* — that than which God can do no greater. The essence of the event of Christ is such that no other religion or culture can add to or surpass the Christian dispensation of salvation. Everything true and good that the other religions contain is a participation in what appeared in its fullness in Jesus Christ.

Still, no man and, indeed, no dogma of the church can ever wholly exhaust this mystery. According to the New Testament, the Spirit of God was promised in order to draw us into this mystery in an ever newer and deeper way (John 16:13).

The encounter with other religions can lead us to see better certain aspects of the unique mystery of Christ. Interreligious dialogue, therefore, is not a one-way street; it is a real encounter that can be an enrichment for us Christians. Here we are not the only ones who have something to give; we also have something to learn and to receive, because in this way we are able to capture in all its length and breadth, height and depth, the fullness of the mystery that was given to us in Jesus Christ (Eph. 3:18).

Both trinitarian theology and Christology, then, give us a prior understanding of unity that is not totalitarian but rather gives space to the other and sets him free. At the very core of love is the fact that it unites intimately, not in order to imprison the other but rather to lead him to his own fulfillment.

These speculative reflections become concrete and practical as soon as we look at the life of Jesus. He is, as the Gospels attest, a man for others; he, the Lord, came not to dominate, but to serve and to offer his life "for the many" (Mark 10:45 and par.). He emptied himself to the point of death, was exalted, and now sits as Lord of the universe (Phil. 2:6-11). In this way, through Jesus Christ, service that consumes and sacrifices itself becomes the new law of the world.

Thus understood, the affirmation of the unity and uniqueness of the Christian dispensation of salvation is not an imperialism that swallows up, co-opts, or oppresses other religions. Even less does it underwrite an imperialistic understanding of mission. It has nothing to do with conquering the world, even if it has often been abusively misunderstood in this sense.

If the unity and uniqueness of the Christian dispensation of salvation is understood in its universal significance, then its global claim also guarantees and defends the inalienable right of every freedom. Precisely in its concrete situation of having already decided (H. Schlier), which is opposed to any sort of syncretism and relativism, it not only lays the foundation for tolerance and respect but also establishes a dialogical and diaconal relation to the other religions — a far cry from any narrow-minded fundamentalism.

This dialogical and diaconal attitude has three aspects. Christianity gives its assent to, respects, and defends all that is true, good, noble, and holy in other religions (Phil. 4:8) *(via positiva seu affirmativa);* it criticizes prophetically whatever in them is detrimental to the honor of God and the dignity of man; it critiques any improper mingling of the divine and the human that detracts from the dignity of both *(via negativa seu critica et prophetica);* finally, Christianity wishes to invite other religions to reach their own fullness and their own fulfillment by placing faith in Jesus Christ and sharing in his fullness *(via eminentiae).* Vatican II's decree on mission sums up all three dimensions when it says: all that is good and true in humanity's religions finds in Jesus Christ its greatest unity and should be critically measured by him, purified by him, and brought to its fulfillment in him *(AG, 9).*

Everything was created for Jesus Christ (Col. 1:16; cf. 1 Cor. 8:6), and everything is to be recapitulated in him (Eph. 1:10). This "everything" reaches far beyond the sphere of the religions; it includes all of reality and places it under the one measure of Jesus Christ and of the service of him who strips and empties himself "for the many." Thus understood, the Christian profession of faith, whose concretely universal claim is scandalous to so many, is a call to, and a foundation of, mutual tolerance and respect, sharing and communication, exchange and reciprocity, understanding, reconciliation, and peace. It leads back to him in whom "all the aspirations of history and culture converge," who is the "central point of humanity, the jewel of hearts and the fulfillment of every heart's desire" (*GS*, 45) — to him "who is our peace" (Eph. 2:14).

The Epistemological Basis of a Theology of Religions

GERHARD LUDWIG MÜLLER

The Plausibility Advantage of the Pluralistic Theology of Religions

The theory that has become known under the name of "pluralist theology of religions" and is championed by John Hick, Paul Knitter, and others reflects the secularized and post-Christian world of the civilizations of Europe and North America.[1]

The average participant in a discussion about religion — be it on a talk show, in an academic context, or in a more intimate setting — most likely takes it for granted that behind the appearance of differing belief systems and ritual practices, all religions come down to the same thing: finding one's true self before the Absolute, which, although unknowable, can still be experienced in some way. Those who, despite their skepticism of metaphysics and impatience with religious superiority complexes, nonetheless find the church in some way interesting are more often than not convinced that the whole point of religious truth claims is ultimately to

---

1. A general overview of the sources of and the literature regarding the pluralist theology of religions is offered by P. Schmidt-Leukel in *Theologische Revue* 89 (1993): 354-70. R. Bernhardt draws the conclusion of a total destruction of the Christian creed in his article "Deabsolutierung der Christologie?" in *Der einzige Weg zum Heil? Die Herausforderung des christlichen Absolutheitsanspruchs durch pluralistische Religionstheologien*, ed. M. von Brück and J. Werbick (Freiburg, Basel, and Vienna, 1993), 144-200.

motivate ethical behavior toward one's fellow man. The main job of the religions is to promote world peace and to help the individual human person to "see beyond" his limited experience. We also hear the argument that since finite human reason (supposedly) cannot verify truth claims about the transcendental, but only about the empirically accessible or the operations of formal logic, there is no viable criterion for checking the cognitive value of religious truth claims. Such claims are thus mere functions of the path to salvation on which all forms of human religiosity are based. No individual religion can demonstrate its superiority over others, much less its exclusive claim to truth, at the bar of reason. According to a certain epistemology, human reason cannot go beyond the limits of its finitude and the severe restrictions placed on its rational knowledge of the ultimate end. This seems altogether plausible and irrefutable to the majority of post-Enlightenment Westerners, who take for granted the fundamental hypothesis of Kant's critical metaphysics. Therefore every religious claim to make absolutely valid statements to the effect that God is a real person who does not merely appear to us as such, or that he reveals himself in a dialogue between the divine and the human, is absolutely unacceptable. It seems to be an arbitrary absolutization of a merely relative uniqueness based on one point of view among others. Indeed, the truth about God cannot be known; God remains unknown.

The peaceful coexistence of people of different religious traditions within a society or a state can be guaranteed only on the condition that all absolute and exclusive claims to the truth of one's own faith in God, the divine, or the transcendental horizon of all worldly experience be abandoned. This is the only way to bring peace among religions, a peace that is in turn necessary to secure a universal and eternal peace among human beings throughout the whole world.

It seems to be a necessary, infallible condition of peaceful coexistence that the followers of different religions recognize the unknowability of the Absolute and the impossibility of any revelation of a personal God. The rejection of the absolute truth claims advanced by particular religions becomes, paradoxically, an absolute claim based on the absolutization of the subjectivity of the *finite* spirit. In an unprecedented reversal of all logic, the finitude of the human spirit becomes an absolute barrier to the infinite.

Hegel, writing in 1802, blamed empiricist anthropocentrism for this incapacity to recognize the transcendental world: "Since the standpoint that omnipotent time and its culture have fixed for reason is that of a reason stimulated by the senses, such philosophy cannot search for knowledge of God, but only of man. This man and this humanity represent the standpoint of such a philosophy, that is, a fixed and insuperable limitation of reason, not as a reflection of eternal beauty, as the focal point of the universe, but as an absolute sensibility, which commands faith by clothing itself in the suprasensible it claims is unknowable."[2]

This fundamental current of skepticism and agnosticism is nourished by other factors as well. There seems to be nothing standing in the way of a destruction of the foundations of a theological theory of an analogous but real knowledge of the existence of the personal God and of his historical-eschatological revelation that occurs in the dialogue between the divine word and faith.

In this sense the exponents of the pluralist theology of religions attempt to revive, and to work into their system, the skeptical-agnostic prejudices of modern Western historiography and its stereotypical examples of religious intolerance based on historical-eschatological claims. We can do no more here than refer briefly to just some of the many mutually reinforcing currents that make of the modern critique of Christianity a maelstrom that threatens to drown the church's creed in the open sea of a universal religion without any compass or landmark in space and time.

The most important of these currents is the dualism between spirit and sense that goes back to Descartes. This dualism gives rise to a self-contradictory philosophy of pure reflection that, on the one hand, mirrors only the formal operation of reason and, on the other hand, is limited to a merely descriptive science of nature, history, and society. Once the unity of man's body and spirit radically is ruptured, there is no longer any intrinsic harmony between man's orientation to transcendence and his concrete communion with God's historical action and incarnate Word.

Reflecting this rationalistic assumption, Baruch Spinoza argued that the incarnation was inconceivable and, therefore, ontologically impossible. By the same token Spinoza regarded the logical expression of the incarnation, that is, the doctrine of the hypostatic union, to be as absurd as the claim that "the circle took the form of a square."[3] Since for Spinoza it is

---

2. G. W. F. Hegel, *Glauben und Wissen oder die Reflexionsphilosophie der Subjektivität in der Vollständigkeit ihrer Formen als Kantische, Jacobische und Fichtische Philosophie* (Hamburg, 1962), 11.

3. Letter 73, to Heinrich Oldenburg, in Baruch de Spinoza, *Briefwechsel* (Hamburg, 1986), 277.

completely unreasonable to hold that belief in an incarnation is necessary for salvation, he considers Jesus to be nothing more than a particularly clear representation of the Son of God, by which he means "the wisdom that has proclaimed itself in all things, especially the human mind and, among all human beings, especially in Jesus Christ."[4]

It goes without saying that empiricism (Hume), sensualism (Baron Holbach), and the positivist critique of metaphysics (the Vienna School and, in part, analytic philosophy) regard the Christian creed as devoid of any claim to truth because it is based on a historical event. Where religion is not understood chiefly as a tool of power wielded by a priestly caste or as an illusion (Feuerbach, Comte, Marx, Nietzsche, Freud), functionalism accords the creed at best a heuristic value as a series of images, poetic metaphors, or incentives to moral behavior (Strauss, Jung, Drewermann). Of course, there is no reality on which the metaphor is based or to which it leads.

Another milestone in the pluralistic theology of religions is Kant's critique of reason. Because theoretical reason is powerless to know the truth and reality of God in his historical manifestation, there remains only a moral faith in God. At best, God is either an ideal derived from theoretical reason or the absolute foundation of moral behavior. In this context natural religion (already developed by the seventeenth-century English freethinkers) is the measure of the Christian teaching on revelation. His inability to bridge the gap between reason and sensation makes Kant unable to secure any intrinsic link between a rational religion of morality on the one hand, and the historically based faith of Christianity on the other. The church's teaching, which makes revelation present, cannot lay any claim to be a faith revealed by God: "It is thus necessary to acknowledge and respect universal human reason as the supreme principle governing both natural religion and Christian doctrine, while loving and cultivating revealed doctrine, on which the Church is founded and which requires scholars as its interpreters and custodians, as the only, albeit invaluable means of making religion understandable even to the ignorant and of assuring its propagation and continuity."[5]

Kant, like the pluralist theology of religions after him, denies that Christ is the one and only mediator of salvation and that the creed of the

---

4. Spinoza, 277.

5. I. Kant, *Religion innerhalb der Grenzen der blossen Vernunft*, in *Kant's Gesammelten Schriften*, vol. 6 (Berlin, 1914), 165.

church and membership in it are necessary means of salvation, while reducing religion to the soteriological and practical:

> The true and only religion contains nothing but laws, that is, those practical principles of whose absolute necessity we can become aware, and which we recognize to have been revealed by pure reason (and not empirically). Certain statutes, that is, supposedly divine prescriptions that, from the point of view of pure moral judgment, are arbitrary and contingent, may be introduced solely for the use of a church, of which there can be different, but equally valid forms. Therefore, to believe in this statutory faith (which in any case is restricted to a certain people and which cannot contain universal religion) as if it were essential to the worship of God as such, and to make it the supreme condition of man's pleasing God, is a *religious illusion,* whose practice is a *false cult,* that is, an imaginary adoration of God that acts against the true worship that God himself has required of us.[6]

A further contribution is the young Schleiermacher's attempt to base religion upon a "feeling of total dependence on the Absolute." Rejecting both early Christianity's metaphysical transmutation of the creed and the Enlightenment's reduction of Christianity to a moral banality, Schleiermacher endeavors to give an account of the Christian faith in terms of an experience of unity with the infinite, which, in his view, appears variously in the finite. On this basis, he argues, Christianity can be called the supreme instance of the presence of the infinite in the finite and the integration of all particular religions. Now Christianity characteristically unites a sense of the immediacy of God with a sense of his mediation in the history of salvation. It is just this unity that Schleiermacher seems to miss — if, in fact, the finite is merely a space for the representation of the infinite, which, remaining uncreated, effaces the historical reality of the individual.

> The fundamental intuition of all positive religion is in itself eternal, because it is an integral part of an infinite totality in which everything must be eternal. But positive religion itself and its whole organization are transitory. . . . Christianity is superior to all of these religions. It is both more historical and more humble in its nobility. It thus explicitly

6. Kant, 167f.

acknowledges its essential transitoriness; the time will come, it tells us, when we will no longer speak of a mediator, but the Father will be all in all. But when will that time come? I fear that it is beyond all time. But if there will always be Christians, may it be that Christianity will be infinite by reason of a universal propagation? Is it alone destined to rule as man's only form of religion? It scorns this despotism; it has enough respect for each one of its elements to rejoice to see it as the center of a whole in its own right; it not only wants to generate an infinite diversity within itself, but also wants to see this diversity outside of itself. Never forgetting that the best proof of its eternity lies in its own corruptibility, in its own sad history, and always awaiting a redemption from the very wretchedness by which it is weighed down, it is glad to see other, younger forms of religion being born all around it, outside of this corruption — religions that seem to it to be on the furthest, most dubious confines of religion in general. The religion of religions can never gather enough material to satisfy its most characteristic intuition and, as there is nothing more irreligious than to demand uniformity in humanity in general, so there is nothing less Christian than to seek uniformity in religion.[7]

The pluralist theology of religions claims support from the historical-critical method, inasmuch as the latter supposedly bases Christian faith on a general experience of the divine, or on a vague transcendence, instead of on the concrete encounter with God in the midst of history. Following Lessing, the pluralists attempt to sift the "religion of Christ" from the "Christian religion." There seems to be a permanent gulf between the "Jesus of history" and the "Christ of faith." The synoptic Gospels allow us to reconstruct the self-understanding of the historical Jesus, which differs considerably from the language his Jewish and Hellenistic followers put into his mouth to express his importance as the catalyst of a religious experience of the absolute and the infinite that utterly transcends human concepts. Because Jesus never explicitly called himself "Son of God," "Eternal Word of the Father," "Messiah," and "Universal Mediator of Salvation," because he refused identification with God, and therefore forbade his own divinization and absolutization, the aforementioned terms call for reinterpretation in a mythical and metaphorical sense. Taken literally, these terms fly in the face of Jesus' own understanding of who he was. In the same way

---

7. D. F. E. Schleiermacher, *Kritische Gesamtausgabe*, vol. 12, *Über die Religion* (Berlin/New York, 1955), 295-97.

a literal reading of the dogmas of Nicea and Chalcedon contradicts the laws of reason. An incarnation is a priori impossible, because the Absolute cannot become finite without losing its divinity. Conversely, no human person can become the appearance, indeed, the personification of God in the Christian sense without losing his human nature. In the end we have the same relativization of Christ, whether, with John Hick, we see Jesus as one of many a posteriori responses to the a priori experience of the Absolute, or whether we join Paul Knitter in understanding Jesus as a man in whom the unconditional demand of the Absolute reaches us through the mediation of a limited human being — even as this mediation is not based on the identification of the subject of Christ's humanity with the hypostasis of the divine Logos. Jesus is something like the closest historical approximation to the supratemporal idea. He may thus be the noblest embodiment of an ideal, but not the incarnation of the real word of God. The pluralists do not venture the step toward the biblical profession that "Jesus *is* the Christ." This means that two thousand years of Christian faith are based on a grave error, while the true essence of Christianity comes to light only through a historical-literal reconstruction. On the other hand, if all religions are manifestations of God, one has to wonder how such a mistake could have happened.

The "advantage" of all this, of course, is that the disagreeable concreteness of the church's profession of faith need no longer trouble the majority of our contemporaries, including socialized Christians, for whom it appears incompatible with scientific, historical, and philosophical reason. General experiences of the Absolute do not challenge people like a concrete confession of faith that may lead them to the point of martyrdom. In a post-Christian society the attraction exercised by the monastic religions of Asian origin is reinforced by a reflexive preference for seeking the truth over finding it and by a distaste for the Christian insistence that the person stands before reality and before God. There is no engagement with the challenge of a personal, historically present God. The exponents of pluralist theology confuse Christianity's absolute claim to truth with a desire to possess the truth in order to boast before others who do not yet possess it. In reality the opposite is the case: the believer considers himself belonging to Christ, for whose sake he has assumed the task of servant of the gospel for the Gentiles (Rom. 15:16) and collaborator with the truth of God (1 Cor. 3:9; 3 John 8).

Giving a positive twist to Feuerbach's theory of projection, the repre-

sentatives of pluralist theology hold that by setting aside a literal understanding of the credo, Christians can reinterpret doctrines that have with-
ered under criticism as culturally conditioned images and expressions of
an experience of the Absolute — and in so doing, make them palatable to
the enlightened who find them offensive. The virgin birth, for example, is
the symbol of an immediate beginning of religious consciousness stem-
ming from the experience of the divine ground of the world. The bodily
resurrection of Christ is a metaphor for hope in something beyond death,
say, the immortality of the soul, or the fusion of the "I" with the undifferentiated "One," or some analogous symbol drawn from one religious tradition or the other. The Trinity, too, is nothing but an ideal abstraction of
the alternation of unity and plurality in which the human spirit finds fulfillment in its striving for the infinite.

The pluralist account also bears certain echoes of Troeltsch, who is oc-
casionally invoked as the father of the pluralistic theology of religions.
Troeltsch sought to transcend both Hegel's retrieval of the finite as a moment in the self-achievement of the infinite and the decisionistic absolute
invested in some historical process or figure (as in "supernaturalism").
Troeltsch's aim, of course, was to find an inductive path into the truth of
religion, which, in his view, has gradually unfolded in history, finally
reaching its (relatively) absolute apex in Christianity. This comparative account of religious truth allows us to see every historical religion as mediat-
ing a certain experience of the divine Absolute, so long as the adherents of
the religion in question not only hold it to be true and worship accordingly, but also live it practically. The profession of dogmatic faith, the self-
donation of God worked by the Holy Spirit, are merely the changeable instrument of this experience of the Absolute, which is ahistorical. It is not a
constitutive dimension of the communication between God and man by
means of which, on the Christian understanding of God's truth and of his
option for us, human beings take part in the relation of love between Father and Son in the Holy Spirit.[8]

Pleasant book titles such as *One God — Many Paths to Salvation* or
God Has Many Names offer easy guidance amidst the disconcerting multiplicity of religions and remove the burden of having to adopt one religion's
claim as truer than another's. The contrast between the beauty of a color-

---

8. E. Troeltsch, *Die Absolutheit des Christentums und die Religionsgeschichte* (1902; Munich and Hamburg, 1969).

ful flower garden and the uniform monotony of an all-Catholic world introduces an aesthetic note into the discussion and thus assures the pluralist conception of religion an advantage in plausibility.

The pluralist theology of religions exploits the supposedly disastrous consequences of Christian absoluteness and, more precisely, of Christology in order to gain a final advantage in plausibility. "Absolutization," as used in this context, does not mean the tact of recalling the Absolute in the "medium" of the finite, but the identification of a finite thing with the Absolute. The incarnation is not the self-communication of God in the finite human nature of Jesus assumed by the hypostasis of the Word, but rather the divinization of Jesus' human nature. There is a putative relationship of cause and effect between the avowal of the uniqueness of Jesus Christ's mediatorship of salvation and the crimes committed under Christian domination of European and world society. A literal understanding of Christ's preexistence, incarnation, and divine Sonship supposedly led to Christian anti-Semitism as well as to violence against heretics. A triumphalist understanding of the church, expressed in the phrase *extra ecclesiam nulla salus,* contributed to violent evangelization and to European colonialism and, therefore, the suppression and destruction of indigenous cultures and religions. Finally, blame for the interconfessional wars in Christian Europe can be laid upon a dogmatic formulation of saving truth in abstract concepts. Only a decisive departure from a dogmatic interpretation of Christianity, whether exclusivist or inclusivist, can clear the way for the acknowledgment that God is manifested in all religions and that all religions are equal expressions in the religious experience of every man. I leave aside the question as to just how far this account of events can stand up to historical and theological interpretations. My main point is only that certain associations give the pluralist account a plausibility that always puts exact theological argumentation at a disadvantage.

The pluralistic "reconciliation" of all historical religions in a supposedly fundamental religious experience of the Absolute thus appears as the only hypothesis that can account for the relationship of the religions with one another and with the divine, as the only epistemologically and morally defensible religious alternative to an atheistic worldview.

Compatibility with the spirit of the age cannot be the only relevant criterion for theological discussion. What must rather be considered is the extent to which a theory accords with the principles and methods of the confession of the Christian community, the church, which aims to formulate the content of the revelation of God through Jesus Christ. Article 4 of the International Theological Commission's "Christianity and the Religions" (1996) suggests the decisive importance of epistemology: "The theology of religions still has no precisely defined epistemological status." This situation gives rise to one of two fundamental principles — either a pluralistic theology of religions or a Christian theology of religions. In contrast to the former, the latter takes its bearings from the eschatological manifestation of God in his Son Jesus Christ as the offer and the mediator of salvation. On this basis it examines the value of those religions outside the concrete history of salvation in Israel and the community of those who believe in Jesus as the Christ of God.

The pluralistic theology of religions begins with an abstraction from concrete religions and proceeds to speculate on the experience of the reality supposedly underlying all religious phenomena in a realm beyond historical concretion. In this way conceptual possibility becomes the ultimate measure of the reality of the many religious ideas and practices that actually exist.

A Christian theology of religions, by contrast, starts from an acknowledgment of the reality of God, the creator and fulfiller of human beings. It does not turn on a presumed experience of the divine ground of the world, but rather on faith in the historical revelation of God in Israel, which becomes finally, unsurpassably concrete in Jesus, the mediator of salvation for all men.

The reality of revelation allows us to conceive the possibility of incarnation. The premise of this Christian theology of religion is a decision for faith in Jesus Christ. The church's proclamation of, and testimony to, God's universal saving will is addressed to the freedom of every single individual. The Christian faith does not destroy the hope that finds expression in other religions and philosophies. Christian hope in man's fulfillment through God perfects the truths found in nature and in other religions in the unique truth of Christ. These natural and religious truths set the stage for the encounter with Christ (inculturation). Coming to faith in Christ is not a simple, superficial change of religion, but rather the fulfillment, granted freely by God through grace, of the search for truth and salvation.

Contradictions of the Post-Christian
Pluralist Theology of Religion

The pluralist theology of religions claims to offer the best possible account of how the historic religions can interrelate today. The pluralists reject the exclusivism of church teaching prior to the Second Vatican Council or, in the Protestant realm, of Karl Barth, who believed that truth and salvation belong to Christianity alone. The pluralists also insist on the inadequacies of inclusivism, which claims the maximum degree of truth and salvation for Christianity alone while granting only a part of this truth to the so-called other religions, which, because it is a part, tends toward explicit membership in the church. Now this way of talking about "religions" places Judaism, Christianity, Islam, and the others under an a priori or normative concept of religion. In reality one would first have to show that all religions, including Christianity, are born of the same fundamental aspiration of the human spirit toward the Absolute. Clearly the specificity of various historical forms is rendered abstract and is identified with a lowest common denominator that supposedly contains the true nature and core of "religion." The particular historic religions are then claimed to emerge from this abstract nature of religion. Religious founders express their (identical) religious experiences using the means placed at their disposal by their respective cultures, while the social forms of the religions get their shape from the typical beliefs and rites of those same cultures.

Now, because from its very beginnings in the pre- and postpaschal faith of the apostles Christianity does not fit into this interpretation of the origin of religion, it cannot be made compatible with the pluralistic system of religions without a reconstruction that overturns its fundamental principles, leaving "no stone upon the other." The representatives of the pluralist theology of religions presuppose a Western Christian background. They use fundamental concepts shaped by Christianity such as God, revelation, truth, salvation, incarnation, mediator, sin, conversion, redemption, eternal life, and so forth. Within the pluralist hermeneutical system, which differs substantially from that of Christianity, the content of all these terms undergoes a change. If the fundamental principle of Christian theology is *fides quaerens intellectum*, the pluralist theology of religions cannot be called Christian theology because it explains the faith on the basis not of listening to the Word of Christ but of a general experience of the Absolute. This experience has its roots in the religious sense as

interpreted by an autonomous subject. The vast gulf between the hermeneutics of Christianity and the hermeneutics of the pluralists becomes
apparent when we analyze the three axioms of the pluralist theology of
religions, which, in light of this analysis, prove to be self-contradictory.
These three axioms are:

There Can Be No Communication
between God and Man in Word and Deed

The human spirit cannot become a hearer of the Word of God. God cannot communicate with man, adapting his message to the human condition
in the incarnate Word. And thus man is not able to participate in the inner
life of the trinitarian God.[9]

God Cannot Become Incarnate

The term "God" is merely the personification of an apersonal experience
of reality conceived in religious terms. Faith in a personal Absolute, or in
an Absolute that is not "nothingness," is itself an interpretation of this
original experience. Even if God were ontologically a person, an incarnation would be impossible a priori. It would logically contradict God's divinity if, in becoming incarnate, the Creator were at the same time a part
of his creation. The "all" cannot become part of itself. The absoluteness of
God rules out the incarnation.[10] The question of what is meant by the
term "God" remains unanswerable: Is it a cipher for the horizon of religious experience, for the Aristotelian unmoved mover, for one of the gods
of mythology, for the divine watchmaker of Deism, or for Yahweh Elohim,
whose Word was made flesh?

9. An excellent critical presentation of the epistemology underlying Hick's theology of
religion is offered by G. Gäde, *Viele Religionen-ein Wort Gottes. Einspruch gegen John Hicks
pluralistische Religionstheologie* (Gütersloh, 1998). For the consequences that follow from
this epistemology, see K.-H. Menke, *Die Einzigkeit Jesu Christi im Horizont der Sinnfrage*
(Einsiedeln and Freiburg, 1995).

10. See J. Hick, ed., *The Myth of God Incarnate* (London, 1977); John Hick, *The Metaphor of God Incarnate: Christology in a Pluralistic Age* (London, 1993); Hick, *A Christian Theology of Religions: The Rainbow of Faiths* (Louisville, 1995).

Human Nature Cannot Have a Divine Hypostasis

Pluralistic theology does not accept the distinction between essence and person, that is, between the nature of man as body-spirit and his personal being. It uses the individual and his empirical consciousness as the reference point to explain the nature of man and of God made man. Pluralistic theology is thus constrained by its own assumptions to interpret Christology in Apollinarian terms. Confusing Jesus Christ's empirical consciousness with his hypostasis, the pluralists accuse the doctrine of the hypostatic union of substituting Jesus' human awareness with the divine consciousness. The classical doctrine, the pluralists charge, is tantamount to the claim that Jesus was a man with a double consciousness,[11] a man who, so to say, considered himself at once human and divine. Hence the pluralist axiom: "A concrete humanity cannot assume the expression, personification, and infinite form of God without ceasing to be a human nature."[12] An incarnation of God is impossible, because a God become man cannot possibly be a real and complete human being.

This hypothesis leads to the denial of the church's faith in Jesus Christ as the incarnate Word of God. It rests upon the epistemological principle of the impossibility of a personal revelation of God to man. John Hick retrieves Kant's critique of knowledge but transforms it in a radically opposite direction. Kant distinguishes human experience into two separate aspects: the thing in itself and the thing as it appears to the subject, that is, the phenomenon. Hick applies this Kantian distinction to the knowledge of God. The thing in itself is identified with the Absolute, and religious phenomena are identified with the phenomenon. Just as it is impossible to know the thing in itself by means of the phenomenon, it is also impossible to know God by means of the religious phenomena. There is only one experience of the Absolute. It is available in the different religions, but it cannot tell us whether the Absolute is personal or not. For Kant, of course, it would make no sense to speak of an "experience" of God, or to identify the

---

11. An example of this failure to understand the classic doctrine of the two natures, two intellects, and two wills of Christ is offered by P. Schmidt-Leukel, *Grundkurs Fundamentaltheologie. Eine Einführung in die Grundfragen des christlichen Glaubens* (Munich, 1999), 206-22. The unity of the two natures, intellects, and wills is not realized in the human awareness of Jesus, but in the hypostasis of the Logos, who gives existence also to the human nature of Christ with its intellect and will.

12. M. Goulder, ed., *Incarnation and Myth: The Debate Continued* (London, 1979), 63.

thing in itself with God, or to claim a transcendent origin of religion. For Kant's theoretical reason, God cannot be known or experienced, since he cannot be an object of experience.

Hick, however, deduces from Kant's premises that all historical religions are a synthesis between the experience of the Absolute and its interpretation filtered through the categories drawn from the experiencing subject's cultural context. Hick does not simply deny any objective foundation to the experience of an ultimate reality, which, in his view, is capable of being experienced. But the role of the subject in actively transforming the experience of absolute reality into concepts or religious images plays such a decisively constitutive role that an objective conceptualization of ultimate reality is out of the question. Religious concepts are only an asymptotic approach to the experience of absolute reality. The experience of God cannot be transformed into dogmas or religious practices. No one form of knowledge of God can be considered the only valid and exhaustive presentation of the experience of the divine. A peaceful competition or dialogue among religions would help them get clear about their own processes of theological transposition and conceptualization and would contribute toward improving their mode of expressing the content of religious experience. At the same time, it also becomes clear that no affirmation of any faith can ever be anything but relative. The articles of the Christian credo, for example, are not true in themselves. They merely represent in an approximative way one experience of the Absolute. Creedal affirmations merely facilitate the intersubjective communication of the experience of God and serve to bind religious communities together. Theoretical reason cannot decide if any one belief is true in itself or which belief systems might be false in themselves. In the end, the only criterion is ethics.

The ethical criterion is based on the experience of the Absolute as the perception of an absolute claim in action. Every religious man, regardless of the creed to which he adheres, is challenged to free himself from concentration on the "I" and to focus on reality, first of all on the reality of the "Thou," to which he must open himself completely. It seems possible to attain a religious pluralism without superiority complexes or exclusivisms inasmuch as all religions are based on some experience of absolute reality. The creeds of the various religions are not mutually exclusive, because they all present legitimate accounts of the absolute reality and help to motivate ethical behavior.

The consequences of Hick's theory for how we understand the revelation and person of Christ are obvious. Jesus did not consider himself to be the complete manifestation of absolute reality. In his experience of the Absolute, he distinguishes himself radically from God. His life was a supreme interpretation of his religious experience of the absolute reality. In order to distinguish himself from the latter, Jesus described it as "Father." Jesus' interpretation of the Absolute cannot be improved upon, but it does not impede others from expressing their own experience of the same. Jesus' interpretation of God can be called an "incarnation" of God only in a metaphorical and poetic sense. He is one human subject who made human subjectivity transparent to the experience of absolute reality in an exemplary way and who obeyed the ethical exigencies of Absolute Being with his whole existence. The divine presence reaches new heights in Jesus' humanity. Jesus thus becomes the origin of a religious movement and of a community. The disciples, Hick continues, called Jesus "Son of God" — in a metaphorical sense — in order to express faithfully the way he is a catalyst of the experience of absolute reality. But the Christians, influenced by Greek substance metaphysics and by then common mythological divinizations of human beings, transformed Jesus from the metaphorical "Son of God" into the metaphysical "God the Son." The soteriological counterpart of this move is the absolutization of Jesus as the sole manifestation of the absolute reality and as the only mediator of salvation. Gnoseologically, the complete identification of the experience of the absolute with the person of Jesus corresponds to the absolutization of dogma.[13]

According to Hick, then, God cannot authentically manifest his divine Word within man's word. The words, concepts, and judgments of human language cannot be taken up into, and sustained by, the truth and the divine offer of salvation so as to make the word of God present in the word of men (1 Thess. 2:13). Because the eschatological manifestation of the triune God in history and the incarnation of the Word are considered to be impossible a priori, the real incarnation professed by the letter to the Philippians (2:6-11), the prologue of John's Gospel, and the dogmas of Nicea and Chalcedon is supposedly inconceivable. Rationally speaking, the

---

13. This also underwrites the persecution of dissident Christians who in reality may have had the same fundamental experience of Jesus as the mediator of truth and salvation from the Absolute, even while formulating it somewhat differently from the orthodox opinion of ecclesiastical authority.

doctrine of the hypostatic union is self-contradictory. It can be retained only if it is recognized as a poetic metaphor.

Because Jesus did not understand himself to be the incarnation of the Absolute, but radically distinguished himself from God, the classic Christocentrism of the Christian religion also collapses. Once Christianity becomes faithful to Jesus' own theocentrism, it will also become capable of pluralism. If it renounces its claim of the absoluteness of Christ, it will be in a position to retrieve Jesus' self-understanding. The religion of Jesus, in contrast to the religion of traditional Christianity, proves suited to the account of religion developed by the pluralists. All religions point beyond concrete creedal expressions to the common center of reference underlying every experience of absolute reality. They are all different paths leading in equally valid ways to the experience of the Absolute and to the search for wisdom and truth.

The Epistemological Basis of a Theology of Divine Revelation and of Human Religions

The Real Manifestation of God as the Origin of a Theory of Religions

An essentialist or conceptualist metaphysics underlies the epistemology of the pluralists. Thought, the constructor of concepts, is taken to be the measure of the real and the possible. This thought, with its a priori concepts, rules out any knowledge of God through the world. But the theology of Christian revelation presupposes a certain knowledge of God through the world. Otherwise, it reasons, it would be impossible to understand what is meant by the term "God" when we say "God reveals himself." The experience of the world is fundamental for the knowledge of God, because, contrarily to what the pluralists affirm, there can be no direct experience of God. Man's spirit is activated through contact with the sensible world. Even metaphysical knowledge of God begins with the world.

The world can be known as finite, and therefore as requiring an infinite and absolute cause. Through this knowledge of the world's finitude it is possible to come to know God. The word "God" thus does not indicate the correlate of some direct experience of the Absolute, but the radically independent reality that stands over against the world and human subjectivity and on which the world depends entirely as origin and end. This natural knowledge of God shows that man in his spiritual nature is the primary manifestation of God — and that on account of his ability to come to know that God exists. Man does not need the historical religions in order to arrive at such knowledge. These religions are rather a means that either facilitate or limit man's natural openness to the absolute mystery. They are to be understood as expressions of the human spirit. One cannot empirically prove that they contain an experience of God, because there can be no direct experience of the divine. The truth claims and soteriological significance of the religions can be tested theologically only from the point of view of supernatural faith. The beliefs of any given faith or religious orientation cannot be verified by means of the criteria of what a neutral, apparently purely "rational" knowledge takes to be "possible."

The correct way to proceed would be to begin with definite opinions embedded in a concrete profession of faith and then to assess the value of the different creeds they express. Given that we cannot empirically demonstrate that any one religion is the work of God — there is, to repeat, no experience of God as God — the claim that all religions are a manifestation or revelation of God, let alone an incarnation of the divine, amounts to an arbitrary, unverifiable hypothesis. The hypothesis of the pluralist theology of religions is invalidated by the simple fact that we cannot understand any religion from a perspective that somehow transcends the concreteness of history and the world.

There is, however, an anthropological constant that is demonstrably present in all religions without exception: the desire for truth and salvation is integral to man's spiritual nature, but it cannot be fulfilled either partly or entirely within this contingent world. According to the Christian faith, the religions variously express the movement of man's search for, and opening to, God. It cannot be said that Yahweh, the God of Abraham and the Father of Jesus Christ, is merely another name for Vishnu or Zeus. Supposing a natural knowledge of God, we can say that the term "God" refers to the transcendent power manifested through the existence of the world (Rom. 1:19ff.). But the concrete proper name that Judaism and Christianity associate with "God" originates with the supernatural revelation of the name of God in a personal encounter with the Mediator of revelation. The different names of God that figure in the religions express an orientation toward the supreme power. But supposing that God himself

35

makes his name known, he thereby freely manifests how we are to understand the meaning of the word "God." The revelation of God's name in Jesus also purifies the natural knowledge of God from original sin and from all human desires and religious notions. As the revelation of the name of God and as true man, Jesus Christ stands in the middle of the world as the "intersection" between God's descent toward man and man's search for God. In his discourse at the Areopagus, Paul, speaking of the quest of the entire human race for the Creator of heaven and earth in whom every man lives, and moves, and has his being as a creature of God, argues that this quest converges upon one man, Christ, whom God destined to be the judge and savior of all human beings (cf. Acts 17:22-34).

If we take seriously man's existence in history and the historical unity of the human race, there is no longer any room to doubt, as did Celsus, or in a later day, rationalism and Deism, that a historical revelation can be intended for all men. Because human beings form a unity in history, a singular historical event can have universal saving significance. It contradicts nothing in human nature to claim that the historical event of Christ has brought supernatural salvation to all — whether living before, contemporaneously with, or after him. Those who believe in Christ are united historically with those who do not believe in him; the Christian can therefore strive for the salvation of all, the living and the dead. The Christian is not distinguished from others because he possesses the whole truth, or at least a greater part of it. In his pilgrim state the Christian is no different from those who, through no fault of their own, have not yet reached the knowledge of Christ or who unconsciously reject him. The Christian believes in the definitive promise of eternal salvation, even as he knows that it can be lost. What sets the Christian apart is this: the believer is ready, through his service and dedication, to announce, and to bear witness to, God's pro-existence in Christ for the salvation of all. In the place of all, Christ gave himself in response to God's self-communication and he sends out the community of believers to be a sign and an instrument of universal salvation.

Christ did not give the church a share in the mission entrusted him by the Father so that the disciples might save the greatest possible number of people from damnation. It is not the church, but God himself, who has reconciled the world to himself through the gift of his own Son, charging the disciples to announce the word of reconciliation (2 Cor. 5:20). Indeed, this proclamation generates the community of believers that makes God's definitive assumption of the entire creation in Christ sacramentally visible and tangible. The incarnation of God in the one man Christ Jesus and the sacramentality of the church as an effective sign of the intimate union of God with men and of men with one another (*Lumen Gentium,* 1) are two sides of the same coin. The church is a sign that the search for salvation and truth is not in vain, because God has made Christ the foundation of salvation for every person and has given his church to humanity as the "pillar and ground of the truth" (1 Tim. 3:15). Those who do not belong to the church are not, however, ipso facto cut off from salvation. They are oriented to the offer of salvation through their search for truth and the meaning of existence.

The Analogia Entis as the Real Foundation of the Representation of the Word of God in Human Words and of the Interaction between Divine and Human Freedom

Although the pluralists affirm the possibility of experiencing God, they take the finitude of human reason to be irrefutable proof that man is in principle incapable of knowing him. In reality, it is precisely the capacity of human reason that allows God to communicate himself to man and to make him a sharer in the trinitarian life.

Knowledge of God is possible by way of the analogy of being. Being actualizes the essence of things, but at the same time it transcends all essences, because it is the universal act of all individual essences. In this way, being opens man's knowledge to the universal and the infinite. Man's knowing is therefore open to God; man can know God and God can make himself known to man. Thus even human words, which express man's knowledge, are open to welcoming the word of God, just as the word of God is not diminished by the human word. God can reveal himself definitively.

The pluralistic theology of religions wants to make Christianity capable of pluralism. Given its epistemological premises, this means rejecting as impossible the self-revelation of God, the Trinity, the incarnation, real knowledge of God, and loving participation in the communion of the Trinity.

By contrast, those who believe in the Bible's testimony to the action of God in history and who acknowledge the disciples' confession of Jesus infer the possibility of revelation from what they see as its accomplished reality.

Faith is not opposed to reason, but reason enlightened by faith under-stands that faith perfects reason.

In like manner the humanity of Christ finds its full self-realization in its union with the Logos, because union with God is the fulfillment of the human being. Therefore the incarnation does not diminish humanity but, on the contrary, elevates and perfects it. In this way man's capacity to know and to desire God also finds its fulfillment in union with Christ.

The doctrine of the hypostatic union is not the mythological absolutization or divinization of a man, but rather displays the fulfillment of man's being in union with God himself.

Faith in Christ opens us up to this fulfillment realized in Jesus, who has shown himself as the way, the truth, and the life (John 14:6).

Christology and Truth

Contemporary Christology in Light of the Question of Truth

MARCELLO BORDONI

The greatest challenge facing Christology today is posed ever more sharply in the context of interreligious dialogue. The challenge arises from an increasing awareness that "Christianity's relationship to the religions of the world has become an intrinsic necessity for faith."[1] Now, this relationship has to do with a central aspect of the religious sense: the question of truth and freedom, of the duty to follow an upright conscience in order to "seek and obey the truth."[2] The proper link between truth and freedom has not always been maintained. This failure is due primarily to an ambiguous conception both of metaphysical truth (that is, insofar as truth is light for the mind) and of the revealed truth that underlies Christianity's claim to uniqueness among the religions. *Now, the freedom that decides for faith cannot be neutral with respect to truth.*

One root of the challenge to the uniqueness of Christianity posed by so-called theocentric pluralism is a metaphysical and epistemological crisis of the concept of "truth." This crisis stems from "conceptual models" that underwrite a rupture between "metaphysical reason" and "hermeneutical reason," a rupture that favors a relativistic understanding of

---

1. J. Ratzinger, *Il Nuovo Popolo di Dio* (Brescia, 1971), 391-92.
2. John Paul II, *Ai rappresentanti delle diverse religioni*, Assisi, 27 October 1986, 2; A. Scola, "I principi del dialogo interreligioso nella teologia cattolica," in *L'unico e i molti, la salvezza in Gesù Cristo e la sfida del pluralismo*, ed. P. Coda (Rome, 1997), 207.

"meaning"[3] for us[4] and that jeopardizes freedom inasmuch as it cannot keep pluralism from collapsing into religious relativism.

According to the International Theological Commission's document "Christianity and the Religions" (1996), the epistemological rupture that undergirds theocentric pluralism is inherited from Kant's dichotomy between "noumenon" and "phenomenon." In fact, because "God, or the Ultimate Reality, is transcendent of, and inaccessible to, man, he or it can be experienced only on the level of a phenomenon clothed in culturally conditioned images and notions; it follows that different representations of the same reality are not necessarily mutually exclusive *a priori*." "The result is a radical separation of the Transcendent, the Mystery, the Absolute, from its representations: 'since all such representations are relative, because imperfect and inadequate, none can lay claim to exclusive truth.'"[5]

The epistemological relativity described by the International Theological Commission is a sort of cloud hanging over interreligious dialogue; *it tends to reduce the truth of religion to a secondary matter and separate it from the question of the soteriological value of religion.* Hence the rather widespread tendency to diminish or relativize the "truth question" in the context of dialogue and to assert that each religion has its own peculiar "criteria of truth." Because of this, there is an ever growing shift toward "pragmatism":

> The religions ought to leave aside their interminable controversy about truth and recognize that their true essence, their true spiritual aim, lies in an orthopraxy that, once again, appears to be an obvious *desideratum* given the challenges of our time. In the end, orthopraxy would be nothing more than service of peace, justice, and the integrity of creation. The religions could keep their beliefs, forms, and rites, but would have to direct them towards orthopraxy. "By their fruits shall ye know them." All religions could thus maintain their own practices; all controversy would become superfluous, and they would all find the unity required to meet the challenges of the day.[6]

3. M. Bordoni, "Riflessioni introduttive," in *Il sapere teologico ed il suo metodo*, ed. I. Sanna (Bologna, 1993), 20ff.

4. K.-H. Menke, *L'unicità di Gesù Cristo nell'orizzonte della domanda sul senso* (Cinisello Balsamo, 1999), 87ff., 133.

5. International Theological Commission, "Christianity and the Religions" (1996), 14.

6. J. Ratzinger, "Il dialogo delle religioni e il rapporto tra Ebrei e Cristiani," in Ratzinger, *La Chiesa, Israele e le religioni del mondo* (Cinisello Balsamo, 2000), 61.

Christology and the Problem of Truth

The crisis of the *metaphysical* dimension of reason shows up especially in the difficulty surrounding the problem of reconciling the "principle of truth," the "historical and cultural conditioning of human thought," and the "multiple forms of religious experience."[7] On account of this crisis, judgments about religious affiliation are freighted by a confusion between "being in the truth" and "being saved." This confusion stands in sharp contrast to the characteristically Christian understanding of "salvation as truth" and "being in the truth as salvation."

The abandonment of the principle of truth is, as noted above, a consequence of the conviction that the mystery of the Absolute is unattainable in itself, that it cannot be uniquely captured by any form of religious experience. Each religion, then, is merely a variety of what the others are, a variety that is simply one among many. *No religion can claim absolute uniqueness with respect to the others.* A claim to uniqueness is acceptable only if "uniqueness" means the "purely historical singularity" to which every historical fact may lay claim insofar as, concretely, it happens only once. But it can go no further than this. Thus "every religion, compared with all the others, is unique. Indeed, it makes no sense to speak of an absolute unicity."[8] We can therefore claim a perfect equality among all religions — and deny any pretension to "singular, absolute truth."

The very historical particularity of the "manifestation of God in Jesus teaches us that no particular historical thing can be considered absolute; the relativity present in Jesus means that every human creature can find God even outside of Jesus, that is, in our worldly history and in the numerous religions that it has spawned. The risen Jesus himself points beyond himself to God. We can even say that God, through Jesus Christ and the Spirit, points to himself as Creator and Redeemer — to the one God of humanity. God is absolute. No religion is."[9]

This passage illustrates the tendency *not only to disregard the meta-*

---

7. This question has already been posed with regard to theological science (see K.-H. Menke, cited in n. 4 above) and the structure of statements of faith. It reemerges here with respect to the problems of experience and of interreligious dialogue.

8. E. Schillebeeckx, "Universalité unique d'une figure religieuse historique nommée Jésus de Nazareth," *Laval théologique et philosophique* 50 (1994): 265; Schillebeeckx, *Umanità. La storia di Dio* (Brescia, 1992).

9. Schillebeeckx, *Umanità*, 219.

physical dimension of truth as a mere product of Western European culture,[10] *but to neglect the truth claim that characterizes the "essence of Christianity" and is based on the personal incarnation of the Son of God in time. This event implies, in fact, a completely new kind of historical singularity entitled to claim true universality.* The urgency of this affirmation imposes itself insofar as we take seriously the unavoidable duty of a theology of religions to "search for a criterion for the truth of religions"[11] and "to commit ourselves to an understanding and evaluation of Christianity in the context of the *de facto* plurality of religions."[12]

Contemporary Epistemologies of Truth

The question, and the valuation, of truth are evolving today in multiple directions. Here I would like to recall briefly some representative forms of contemporary epistemology. Some thinkers emphasize the *more existential or "living" aspect* of truth; they thus adopt Blondel's principle of the immanence of *"truth"* as an *adaequatio realis mentis et vitae.* Others highlight the *structurally dialogical character* of truth, the knowledge of which necessarily involves otherness and freedom. Still others, finally, insist on the *mythological nature* of truth, especially of religious truth.

Truth in the Sphere of Lived Experience and Interiority

There is a tendency in contemporary thought to privilege the *more existential aspect* of truth along with the *principle of interiority.* In this tendency

10. F. Wilfred, "Some Tentative Reflections on the Language of Christian Uniqueness: An Indian Perspective," in *"Pontificum Consilium Pro Dialogo inter Religiones" Bulletin* 85-86 (1994): 1-2, 57, argues that the question of the uniqueness of Christianity is a purely Western and European debate between dogmatists — whether of reason or of faith — and liberal reactionaries who attempt to relativize this uniqueness. According to Wilfred, the language employed in the debate presupposes an epistemological background that cannot be assumed to be valid for other cultures.

11. International Theological Commission, "Il cristianesimo e le religioni," in *La Civiltà Cattolica* 148 (1997), 1:151; see also 148.

12. P. Ciardella, "Verità e dialogo interreligioso. Alcune considerazioni folosofiche," in *Il pluralismo religioso. Una prospettiva interdisciplinare,* ed. A. Fabris and M. Gronchi (Cinisello Balsamo, 1998), 143.

the point of reference is the *experience of the subject and his fidelity to what conscience reveals to him about the requirements for salvation*. *Veritatis Splendor* warns against replacing the "principle of truth" in "moral judgment" with a radical subjectivization of conscience. The result of such subjectivization, the encyclical tells us, is that "the unavoidable necessity of seeking truth is replaced by a criterion of sincerity, authenticity, of 'fidelity to oneself.' In the end, this tendency leads to a radically subjectivistic concept of moral judgment" (32). *The same tendency is now extended to the (subjective) value of membership in a given religion*. But if the Ultimate Reality of different religions is identical, it does not matter *how* any particular religion contacts the absolute foundation *(the principle of truth, God in himself, is inaccessible to man)* and *how* God is manifested in human experience. It follows that "all religions are relative, not because they tend towards the Absolute, but in all that they say and do not say."[13]

Hence the invitation to Christianity to abandon the principle of the absoluteness of truth and to adopt a more experiential, existential, subjective criterion that will supposedly free it from the ideology that freights its claim to superiority over other religions. But to accept this invitation, as *Fides et Ratio* (hereafter *FR*) tells us, is to fall into a relativism that leads to a progressive "crisis of consciousness." Indeed, the human spirit, absorbed by an ambiguous form of thought, ends up "withdrawing even more into itself, within the limits of his own immanence, with no reference to the transcendent" (*FR*, 81). *Religious experience, enclosed within the limits of a radical immanence, risks being reduced to a mere phenomenon.*

There are numerous attempts to make good on the claim that a phenomenology "of immanence" or of interiority is the only path to the absolute.[14] Such attempts seek to secure transcendence directly from within immanent interiority. To take one well-known example, Michel Henry uses this type of method to elaborate a renewed philosophical understanding of Christianity in the face of the irreversible crisis of modernity and of

---

13. International Theological Commission, "Il cristianesimo e le religioni," 16.

14. "Immanence constitutes the inmost nature of the absolute, the absolute itself, its essence. The absolute itself is therefore conceivable on the basis of this hidden state and as that which is manifested in it" (M. Henry, *L'essence de la manifestation*, 2nd ed. [Paris, 1990]). See G. Lorizio, "Interiorità. La via dell'immanenza," in Lorizio, "Attese di salvezza in alcune figure del pensiero 'post-moderno,'" in P. Coda, ed., *L'unico e i molti*, 19-28; G. Sansonetti, "La fenomenologia dell'invisibile di Michel Henry," preface to *Io sono la verità. Per una filosofia del cristianesimo*, by M. Henry (Brescia, 1997).

the realization that the notion of truth itself has become more problematic and uncertain than ever before. Henry opens his discussion of the meaning of (philosophical) "truth" by refusing to pose the question "whether Christianity is true or false," and by asking instead "what Christianity regards as truth," in other words, the truth that Christ claimed to be (John 14:6). But Henry thus fuses philosophy and Christology. There is, in his view, a structural link between phenomenology and theology. In virtue of this link the theological question of truth tends to become identical with the phenomenological question. "Theology is possible only as phenomenology"; phenomenology is about the manifestation of things, not "what is given or made known, but solely in its mode of being given."[15]

Once this fusion has occurred, *the question of truth quickly proves to be of limited importance.* This is especially the case if in trying to determine what it means to say that "Christ is the truth," one refuses, like Henry, to define the "truth of Christianity" in terms of history, by which he means that the *texts of the Christian tradition do not relate any factual truths.*[16] But granting that historical argumentation alone cannot ground the "truth of faith," can we therefore say that a "phenomenological understanding" is a sufficient, or indeed, a "necessary" method? To answer in the affirmative is of course to submit the concept of Christian truth to a typically modern analysis.

Certainly the idea of interiority as an access to truth is an important one that is authoritatively enshrined in the tradition of Christian thought.[17] Yet, while the appeal to interiority underscores the revelatory action of God in the depths of the heart, it also tends, under the influence of the "mystical religions" (Hinduism, Buddhism, Taoism), to a rigorously apophatic account of divine manifestation. As a result, "there is no claim to know the divine; religion is no longer defined in terms of positive content and therefore in terms of sacred institution. It is completely absorbed into mystical experience, which rules out *a priori* any possible conflict with scientific rationality."[18] Thus, in the age of mystical religion, of which the New Age movement is the most disturbing symptom, rationality is defined

15. M. Henry, "Acheminement vers la question de Dieu: preuve de l'être ou éprouve de la vie," *Archivio di Filosofia* 58 (1990): 525.

16. Henry, *Io sono la verità*, 21: "*the truth of Christianity has absolutely nothing to do with the sort of truth that pertains to the analysis of texts or to their historical study*" (Henry's italics).

17. Augustine, *Confessions* 3.6; Bonaventure, *In I Librum Sententiarum*, dist. I, a.3, q.2.

18. J. Ratzinger, "Grandezza e limiti delle religioni mistiche," in Ratzinger, *Il dialogo delle religioni*, 61-62.

precisely as the rejection of every truth claim and, therefore, as the justification of every kind of intolerance. If we push this approach unilaterally, history is emptied of the divine. Salvation is found outside of the world and its history. Once everything is reduced to life, the central theme of the phenomenological tendency, there is no room left for historical manifestation. "We are questioning the very concept of historical truth itself, which is incapable of capturing the reality of individuals and of anything that pertains to them."[19]

Faced with these indications of the importance of the "question of truth" and its profound relationship with Christianity, especially at the end of the second millennium, we could say that the great challenge is "the ability to pass from phenomenon to foundation; this ability is an urgent necessity" (*FR*, 83). This is not to deny, of course, that experience plays an important role in the interiority and spirituality of man. Moreover, it is also true that man's life cannot be reduced to intellect alone, but that it comprehends the heart and the passions. Nevertheless, speculative reflection must be able to attain spiritual substance and the foundation that sustains it.

Truth, Dialogue, and Proclamation

The necessity of dialogue as a way to truth becomes apparent today not only because of an attitude of tolerance, or of a defense of the right to freedom of conscience and, therefore, of religious plurality, *but also because of the conviction that the encounter with "truth" intrinsically includes dialogue.* The church, which lives everywhere in the midst of men of different religions, *increasingly sees dialogue as a necessity* that "leads to love and mutual respect; it eliminates or at least diminishes the prejudices between the followers of the different religions and promotes unity and friendship between peoples."[20] *Fides et Ratio* probes more deeply still: because "the man who seeks the truth is . . . also *the one who lives by faith*" (31), *the search for the truth leads to asserting the necessity, the need for another, on the path to truth.*

19. Henry, *Io sono la verità*, 22.
20. *Christifideles laici*, 30.12.35; *Enchiridion Vaticanum*, XI (Bologna, 1992), 1757.

Marcello Bordoni

Interreligious Dialogue: A Constitutive Aspect of
Christian Faith Based on the Event of the Truth in Person

Interreligious dialogue *today increasingly appears to be an integral part of faith in Jesus Christ and the mission of the church.* Indeed, we can hardly conceive of a Christian faith that is not somehow connected with the religions.[21] This implies the need for a quest for truth that involves different positions. *By the same token, our epistemological model must stress the relationship between truth and dialogue, and therefore the relationship between truth and otherness.* Some observers rightly note that there remains a "justified suspicion that the search for truth and the recognition of otherness are more divergent alternatives than aspects of a single whole."[22] There are thus two opposing distortions of interreligious dialogue. On the one hand, otherness is repudiated and demonized in order to safeguard the absolute value of truth. On the other hand, otherness has been emphasized to the point of doing away with truth. Now there can be no true dialogue that does not take account of the challenge posed by the Christian claim to uniqueness.

Dialogue and the Inescapability of Metaphysics   Arguments for the necessity of dialogue, especially on religious questions, cannot avoid the metaphysical exigencies of truth, particularly today. On the other hand, the need for dialogue leads to a better understanding of these exigencies, insofar as it uncovers a metaphysic that exceeds a merely "substantialist" account of being, a metaphysic centered instead on the "person" and open to a new understanding of being as love.[23] This raises the question of the rela-

21. Scola, "I principi del dialogo interreligioso," 205. Scola cites Ratzinger, *Il Nuovo popolo di Dio*, 391: "the relationship of Christianity with the religions of the world has become today an internal necessity for the faith."

22. A. Russo, "Verità e alterità. Dal Lógos dia-lógos," in *Il Cristo. Nuovo criterio in filosofia e teologia?* ed. A. Ascione and P. Guistiniani (Naples, 1995), 57; G. Cicchese, *I percorsi dell'altro. Antropologia e storia* (Rome, 1999).

23. International Theological Commission, "Teologia, Cristologia, Antropologia," in *La Civiltà Cattolica* 134 (1983): 57: "In the light of the Christian faith, it is possible to draw forth a new vision of the universe as a whole. Even though such a vision submits the striving of today's man to a critical examination, it nonetheless affirms its importance, purifies it and surpasses it. Substance is no longer placed at the center of such a 'metaphysics of charity' as it was in ancient philosophy. Rather, it is the person, whose most perfect act, whose most suitable way to perfection, is charity."

tionship, or the compatibility, between the claims of unity and absolute truth on the one hand and of plurality on the other. This question can be summed up as follows: "can there be a pluralistic, but not relativistic conception of the truth? Are we entitled to affirm a reconciliation of the uniqueness of truth with the multiplicity of its formulations? Can there be a dialogue that presupposes inseparably and simultaneously both the otherness of the partners and the unity of truth?"[24] The key to this problem is not so much the difference between noumenon and phenomenon as the difference between truth as an event manifested in history and as an event centered on the person who manifests himself in his very self-gift, even while communicating himself through the filter of history and interpretation.

Authentic dialogue presupposes *a prior understanding of the human person* as "inclined to truth." Dialogue is, after all, a "common effort of humanity to arrive at the truth" (*FR*, 2). If the truth is a light that enlightens every man, "there must exist a true path that enables every man to seek it. In so doing, it will make every man truly human — but only within the horizon of truth. Outside of this light, man's existence is always subject to doubt and uncertainty, and, therefore, has no meaningful future."[25] *Without a dynamic toward truth, without a metaphysical truth, otherness and plurality will inevitably degenerate into relativism and phenomenologism* (*FR*, 82).

For this reason *Gaudium et Spes* observed that "intelligence . . . is not limited to the sphere of phenomena alone, but can also attain intelligible reality with true certainty, even if, as a consequence of sin, it is partially darkened and debilitated" (*FR*, 15). Today the threat of a predominant "nonmetaphysical phenomenology" calls for a counterweight: "a philosophy of an *authentically metaphysical* range, capable, that is, of transcending empirical data in order to arrive in its search for truth at something absolute, ultimate, and fundamental" (*FR*, 83). This counterweight discloses the authentic horizon in which man searches for truth. This horizon is also the horizon of the *religious quest;* "the search for the truth is a first *vocatio ad credendum.*" "The man who seeks the truth is also one who lives by faith" (*FR*, 31). Indeed, as John Paul II has stated, "when the why of things is investigated with integrity, in search of the ultimate and most complete answer, *human reason reaches its summit and opens to religion.* In fact, religion rep-

---

24. L. Pareyson, *Filosofia dell'interpretazione* (Turin, 1985), 50-51.
25. R. Fisichella, *Introduzione alla lettura della Fides et Ratio* (Casale Monferrato, 1998), 19.

resents the highest expression of the human person, because it is the culmination of his rational nature. It springs from man's profound aspiration for the truth and is the basis of his free and personal search for the divine."[26]

This search for truth, as a response to the *vocatio ad credendum,* also recalls man's need for the other on the path toward truth (principle of dialogue): "It should not be forgotten that even reason needs to be supported, in its search, by a trusting dialogue and a sincere friendship" (*FR,* 33). "The climate of suspicion and distrust that at times surrounds speculative research forgets the teaching of the ancient philosophers, who regarded friendship as one of the most appropriate contexts for correct philosophizing" (33). *The principle that religious truth is dialogical can thus bring together not only those who explicitly reside within the "Christian" horizon of truth,* in which the experience of truth is fulfilled in communion and growth, but also all human beings who explicitly or implicitly *set out on an authentic and sincere search for the truth* in an attitude of acceptance of, and listening to, the truth.

Dialogue, Freedom, Truth, and the Person   This dialogical relationality points us, as I have said above, toward a personal conception of truth. Man, who tends toward truth, is oriented toward a Truth that becomes concrete in a personal Absolute (Absolute Person) who manifests himself to man in his historical self-giving (truth as event). But if interpersonal relation is on its way toward a person who is truth, it necessarily involves freedom and conscience. Within this horizon *love is the decisive entryway to* (the epistemological aspect) *and element of truth* (the ontological aspect: ontology of agape). "Man's perfection does not lie in the acquisition of an abstract knowledge of truth, but rather consists in a living relationship of giving and of fidelity towards the other. In this faithfulness that knows how to give of itself, man finds full certainty and security. At the same time, however, knowledge through belief, which is founded on interpersonal trust, is not without reference to the truth: man, in believing, trusts the truth the other shows him" (*FR,* 32). This relationship of fidelity and of giving to the other seems more "generic and abstract when dealing

26. John Paul II, *Udienza generale dell'Anno Santo. 19 ottobre 1983,* 1-2, in *Insegnamenti,* VI, 2 (1983), 814-15. In *Fides et Ratio,* 33 n. 28, the Holy Father recalls that he has long made this argument and has expressed it on a number of occasions. Cf. Scola, "I principi del dialogo interreligioso," 208 n. 21.

with information or the results of science than when it touches personal intimacy as in the relationship of a baby with its parents or between spouses who promise each other everlasting fidelity. Nevertheless, even generic and daily fidelity remains the expression of that radical and foundational fidelity *('Urvertrauen')* without which no human life would be possible and that is acquired precisely in the most intimate relationships."[27]

Dialogue, Truth, and Testimony   The dialogical relation of communication as a path to truth may be best described in terms of "testimony." Klaus Hemmerle rightly observes that the category of testimony is decisive for understanding not only the truth, but man himself.[28] By essence man is a "witness to the truth." Man is himself in word, language, and dialogue — the very features that are the core of testimony. Among human beings, then, testimony is the quickest path to truth. Franz Rosenzweig goes so far as to state that *testimony to the truth* is the heart of a new "theory of knowledge" that overcomes "desperately static truths such as those of mathematics and the old epistemologies." The way is thus cleared to "reach the truths for which man spares no expense including those that he can assert only by sacrificing his life."[29] *Fides et Ratio* shares this conviction, which suggests the importance of the "testimony of the martyrs" as the most genuine witness "to the truth about existence." For this reason, today no less than in the past, "the testimony of the martyrs fascinates, generates agreement, finds a hearing and a following." Their witness to the point of sacrificing their lives lays before us the evidence of a truth that does not need long arguments to be convincing. The martyr "awakens in us a profound confidence, because he says what we already feel and makes evident what we also would like to find the strength to express" (*FR*, 32).

Interreligious dialogue must be conducted with respect for others' sincere search for the truth offered concretely to man in a common fraternal, dialogical, and testimonial search. The Christian is called to participate in this search, which *tends toward that personal event of truth that gives itself in the Word made man who declares, "I am the truth"* (John 14:6), and testi-

27. Peter Henrici, "La Verità e le verità," in *Per una lettura dell'Enciclica Fides et Ratio* (Vatic7n City, 1999), 81.

28. K. Hemmerle, "Verità e testimonianza," in *Testimonianza e Verità*, ed. P. Ciardella–M. Gronchi (Rome, 2000).

29. F. Rosenzweig, *Kleinere Schriften* (Berlin, 1937), 395ff.

fies to this statement in the supreme dramatic event of the cross (John 18:37; 19:5, 13). To the man who is sincerely searching for the truth and for a Person in whom to trust, the Christian faith holds out the Truth personified in Jesus Christ ("the truth which is in Jesus Christ": Eph. 4:21; Col. 1:15-20). Christ "is" the "truth" (John 14:6) of God, the eternal Word, precisely as *incarnate;* his entire person reveals the Father (*Dei Verbum* [hereafter *DV*], 4). The truth, therefore, which man's mind and heart seek, without being able to know its personal face ("the unknown God": Acts 17:23), can be reached only through Jesus Christ, the fullness of the truth.

The Christian event, illuminating reason, suggests an account of truth that, free from abstraction, coincides with the person of Jesus Christ in his entrance into history through the event of the incarnation.[30] It is the Truth itself, a unique event, which in its manifestation gives rise to dialogue (covenant) by calling the human subject to whom it is manifested. If human freedom is to cooperate *with reason* in consenting to being, "the ultimate structure of the act of consciousness that intends reality has *the form of faith.*" Faith, then, "is not extrinsic to reason, but rather in a certain sense is its truth."[31] We could even say that Christian faith is the graced enactment of this original fiducial structure intrinsic to man's opening up to truth.

Truth as Adequation and Unveiling

Dialogue and testimony suggest that "truth is the saying of being."[32] Thomas adopts the Aristotelian position that the essence of truth is an *adaequatio rei et intellectus,* which he locates in the judgment.[33] The essence of truth consists in the "declaratory act of saying the real as it really is."[34] This logical dimension of truth reflects, however, its ontological foundation "in things" (in their intelligibility), a foundation that makes possible the truth of the intellect, that is, what Thomas calls adequation. We could therefore say the essence of truth involves the intellect's opening

---

30. H. de Lubac, *Opera Omnia: la rivelazione divina e il senso dell'uomo* 14 (Milan: Jaca Book, 1985), 49. In this event of "giving," the truth is "unveiled," even while remaining veiled.

31. Scola, "I principi del dialogo interreligioso," 213.

32. Aristotle, *Metaphysics* 10.1051b6-9.

33. Thomas Aquinas, *De veritate* 1, 3.

34. P. Ciardella, "Testimonianza e verità. Un approccio filosofico," in *Testimonianza e Verità,* 42.

to the perception, in the light of being, of beings in their maximum evidence and intelligibility.[35] *Fides et Ratio* (56, 82) makes its own this concept of truth; according to the encyclical, it is normative for all knowledge, whether theoretical, metaphysical, or practical, the latter being the kind of knowing involved in action, where we "do" in order to "make true."[36]

While we must defend the account of truth as adequation, the generic character of this account does not always seem immediately relevant to one of the most frequent instances of truth, namely, historical truth. It is thus necessary to integrate certain new elements into it. In historical truth the object can be verified only through the "mediation" of either an oral or a written testimony that renders the event present to the subject's judgment. This situation is further complicated for objects we cannot experience either mediately or immediately but have to do with a particular experience of meaning or of interiority. Religious language belongs to the category of testimony. Here the witness is first of all someone who has seen and communicates what he has experienced. An example would be the "truthful testimony" of which the author of the Fourth Gospel speaks in relating how, when Jesus' side was pierced with the lance, blood and water flowed out (John 19:35): "he who saw it has borne witness — his testimony is true, and he knows that he tells the truth, that you also may believe." Because of the link between truth and testimony, we can speak not only of the *historical or factual* "truth" of what is narrated, but also of the *meaningful* truth, that is, the theological truth lying in the depth of the event into which the narrator has penetrated.

This last reflection suggests that truth must have a metaphysical, theological, and religious density, in spite of the postmodern tendency to erase the idea of adequation by silencing being through a denial of its revelatory, epiphanic character as unveiling.[37] "Truth as revelation *(alétheia)* is central for philosophy and theology, because, in addition to divine Revelation, there is a natural word, or a natural aptitude for revelation built into being, which, as 'epiphanic,' is also theo-phanic."[38] It is precisely "truth as revela-

35. Aquinas, *De veritate* 1.

36. V. Possenti, "Verità e pensiero credente. A partire dalla Fides et Ratio," in *Il risveglio della ragione. Proposte per un pensiero credente,* ed. G. Sgubbi and P. Coda (Rome, 2000), 63.

37. The use of this terminology, which suggests Heidegger's critique of the forgetfulness of being, must not be taken as implying that Heidegger's rather ambiguous employment of it is the only legitimate one.

38. Possenti, 61.

tion" that constitutes the ontological truth underlying acts of judgment. We need to bid farewell to forgetfulness of being and all its correlatives — such as postmodern antirealism or subjectivist constructivism. We need to embrace a realism for which the light comes from being, from the object, and knowing is not the spirit's creative, or even primarily interpretive, act, but rather a perception. Although *Fides et Ratio* does not use this language, it emphasizes the substance of it throughout.

The Absoluteness of True Propositions in the Context of Noncontradiction

There is no shortage of philosophers who defend the dialogical principle as an essential component of man's journey toward the truth and yet, while considering themselves Christian, do not take account either of the distinctively Christian perspective on truth or the distinctively philosophical and metaphysical perspective of epistemology. The reason for this failure seems to be that the notion that Christian thought's insistence on metaphysical truth is purely and simply a product of European culture and philosophy. This insistence on truth, grounded on the principle of noncontradiction and on the understanding of truth as adequation, ends up defining truth as opposition to, or exclusion of, every other truth claim. The claim to an absolute, unique truth supposedly rules out dialogue and otherness.

According to this critique, the traditional concept of true propositions ties their truth to uniqueness and absoluteness; true propositions, then, are either exclusive or inclusive of alternative truth claims. This understanding of truth supposedly culminates in Christianity's account of the relationship between religion and truth; Christianity, it is argued, claims truth in such a way as to cast itself as the vertex of a historical process involving all human religions. "Only Christianity, in fact, has the courage to make an absolute claim." This "Eurocentric model of truth" supposedly underwrites the idea of a "true," or "unique," or to speak with German idealism, "absolute" religion.[39]

---

39. H. Waldenfels, *Manuel de théologie fondamentale* (Paris: Cerf, 1990), 296ff. Waldenfels, referring to H. Fies, "Absolutheitsanspruch des Christentums," *Lexikon fürTheologie und Kirche*, 1:71-74; W. Kasper, "Absolutheitsanspruch des Christentums," *Sacramentum Mundi*, 1:39-44; K. Lehmann, "Absolutheit des Christentums als philosophisches und theologisches Problem," in *Absolutheit*, ed. W. Kasper (Freiburg, 1977),

Beyond the Eurocentric Paradigm: Transition to a New Form of Truth Claim
These considerations naturally lead their proponents to advocate a "new model of truth" for epistemology in general and for religious truth in particular. The truth is defined not as something that excludes or absorbs "other truths," but rather as something that "relates" to other truths and grows in a relationship. In short, "the truth" is defined *not by exclusion* but *by relation. No truth should remain alone, no truth should be completely immutable.* "The truth by nature needs other truths . . . , without 'another' truth, the truth cannot be unique, it cannot exist. The truth, therefore, 'proves itself,' not by triumphing over all other truth but by proving its own capacity to interact with other truths, that is, to teach them and to learn from them, to include them and to be included."[40]

Hence the "relational model of truth," which is supposedly better suited to the dialogical structure of truth. Indeed, this *dialogical structure* is not merely a stage on the way toward a single absolute truth, but reflects the fact that every religion has something uniquely and distinctively its own, a particular way of perceiving divine truth *(which in itself is unattainable).* Therefore, without other truth the truth cannot be unique, it cannot exist.[41]

According to its proponents, this new dialogical and relational model of truth has the advantage of "not jeopardizing faith's absolute commitment" while at the same time highlighting the "relativity" of the "truth of Christianity." This relativity is not to be understood in the sense in which the relative is opposed to the absolute, but rather in terms of the *relational form* of truth: "the truth to which Christianity bears witness is neither exclusive nor inclusive of every other truth; it is relative to whatever is true in the other religions."[42] But this type of argument already displays the weakness of an epistemology based on a *shaky metaphysical foundation:* scant

---

13-38, argues that the claim of Christian absoluteness does not originate with theology but with German idealism. According to Waldenfels, it is rooted in Hegel's notion of "absolute religion."

40. P. Knitter, "Dialogo basato su di un nuovo modello di verità," in Knitter, *Nessun altro nome? Un esame critico degli atteggiamenti cristiani verso le religioni mondiali* (Brescia, 1991), 226.

41. W. C. Smith, *The Faith of Other Men* (New York, 1972), 17: "when dealing with ultimate realities, the truth is not found in either-ors, but in both-ands."

42. C. Geoffrey, "La singularity del cristianesimo nell'età del pluralismo religioso," *Forum Theologicum* 6, no. 1 (1992): 45.

attention is paid to the "principle of absolute truth" underlying all partial knowledge of truth and every moment of the dialogical quest for truth.[43] Even if man's knowledge of truth necessarily passes through historical and cultural conditioning, it does not follow that historicism is a tenable interpretation of this necessity. In fact, we need "a hermeneutics open to the metaphysical claim . . . that could show how, from the historical and contingent circumstances . . . we pass to the truth that transcends this conditioning" (*FR*, 95).

Now *this metaphysical weakness is even more apparent when it comes to the theology of Christian "Truth,"* which is a person-event (John 14:6) whose fullness is given by grace and welcomed in faith — not attained primarily by way of "relationship" with partial truths. *Nor is it the goal of a journey on which every religion begins at an equal distance from the absolute truth.* But does it make sense today to insist on the equal "need to avoid, wherever it is found, 'absolutism, as well as relativism'" about the truth? Can a dialogical model of the structure of truth whose epistemology rests upon a weak metaphysics be right in claiming that a principled, and not merely factual, pluralism is somehow necessary to sustain the relationality of truth? It is hard to see how *this way of asserting the "relative value" of Christian truth can avoid religious relativism.*

This approach leads in fact to the following conclusion: "the distance between the ideality of the incarnate Logos and the enactment of truth in contingent history, through Israel, between the life of Jesus and Western culture, limits every claim to exhaustive fullness on the part of Christianity."[44] Hence the desire to eliminate all talk of "absolute truth" and historical "uniqueness": the debate about these issues is supposedly "framed primarily in Western terms as a controversy between dogmatists and reactionary liberals who would relativize uniqueness claims. This language . . . has its assumptions and epistemological background, and there is no guaranteeing that these can be extrapolated to other cultures."[45]

This problem has been seriously tackled by the church, which has *underlined the necessity of dialogue in the context of otherness.* Yet the church

43. "The capacity to seek the truth and to ask questions already implies a first response. Man would not begin to search what he had no knowledge of or esteemed absolutely unattainable" (*FR*, 29).

44. J. S. O'Leary, *La vérité chrétienne à l'âge du pluralisme religieux* (Paris, 1994), 279-80.

45. Wilfred, 1-2, 57.

feels equally the fundamental need to underscore the *indispensable missionary proclamation of truth, without which Christian identity is seriously compromised.* Thus while the church, speaking through the magisterium of the current pope, affirms that dialogue is *intrinsically necessary to the proclamation of the gospel,*[46] it also insists on the need to achieve man's call to unity, which is realized precisely through truth animated by love.[47]

It is therefore necessary to point out the importance of understanding the profound connection between "dialogue and announcement," *first of all by rejecting any separation of the two.* This separation would be injurious to both parties: a "proclamation without dialogue" would risk estranging Christian mission from Christian awareness of being already the "concrete presence of the truth" (who is Christ himself) among men, not only as the self-manifestation of the Father in the Son, but also as the revelation of man's "truth" to himself (*Gaudium et Spes,* 22) in accord with the humanizing power of Christian truth. John Paul II justifies theological dialogue by arguing from the "mystery of unity" that already links[48] Christians and those who are "ordered" to the church. On the other hand, a "dialogue without proclamation" would again risk a relativism of the truth that would overlook the fact that it tends to manifest itself to every man.

In opposition to both these extremes, *we need to maintain in constant tension both the unity and the distinction between dialogue and proclamation.* In this way we express the *already and not yet* of the church in its

46. It is above all with the document "Dialogo e Annuncio" (*Secretariatus pro non christianis, Bulletin* 56; 19 [1984]/2, 166-67) that *it is openly stated that the dialogue among religious faiths is part of the church's mission to evangelize.*

47. For the texts of the magisterium, see F. Gioia, ed., *Il dialogo interreligioso nel magistero pontificio (Documenti 1963-1993)* (Vatican City, 1994).

48. In light of a twofold mystery of unity — the unity based on creation ("there is but one divine plan for each human being that comes into this world") and the unity based on the mystery of the universal redemption of Christ — John Paul II, in his well-known speech to the Roman curia (22 December 1986), affirms the church's duty to work with all its resources (evangelization, prayer, dialogue) to reconcile the divisions between men, which distance them and make them hostile toward one another (6). Cf. M. Bordoni, "Singolarità ed universalità dell'evento cristologico e del cristianesimo nel contesto creativo," in Bordoni, "Singolarità ed universalità di Gesù Cristo nella riflessione cristologica contemporanea," in P. Coda, ed., *L'unico e i molti,* 104f.: "Although the phrase Christological anthropology is not a tautology, it remains true that these two terms must not be juxtaposed. The unity of the two terms attests that, as D. Wiederkehr says, 'the earthly self-revelation of God in Jesus Christ and man's capacity to embody it are intimately ordered to each other.'"

earthly state. If in fact the church is a pilgrim in history, on a "journey towards the fullness of the Kingdom and its Truth" (John 16:13), it uses dialogue in order to become solidary with all of humanity and so to respond to the Holy Spirit prompting us to the know the truth. On the other hand, the church is the "presence, the sacrament of the Kingdom" in the world and in time. She is the repository of truth, which she cannot submit to negotiation and to discussion, but which she can and must only "proclaim."

Truth as "Gratuity" and as "Myth"

Postmodern approaches to truth, like fragments of fundamental human experience, oscillating between the radical invasion of the o/Other and radical interiority,[49] suggest a kind of encounter with truth through gratuity, gift, and self-surrender. The order of the day here is the so-called metaphysics of charity. This, says the International Theological Commission in connection with the metaphysics of charity,[50] is the situation in which "Christian philosophy"[51] finds itself today. To be sure, this approach has the merit of overcoming a substantialistic understanding of metaphysics and thus of moving toward a view of truth that goes beyond a "correspondence" entangled in the webs of "ousiology." On the other hand, an affirmation of agape that would maintain truth without being is less helpful.[52] We must rather rethink being itself as self-diffusive, as gift. To do so is to place being in a context of "agapic love" in which an epistemology of truth flourishes in intimate connection with love.[53] We must, in other words, affirm truth as love "in a way that includes (not: excludes) the horizons both of ousiology and of ontology."[54]

---

49. G. Lorizio, "La via della gratuità. Fenomenologia del dono e 'metafisica della carità,'" in Lorizio, "Attese di salvezza in alcune figure del pensiero post-moderno," in *L'unico e i molti*, 28-34; Lorizio, *Rivelazione cristiana, Modernità Post-modernità* (Cinisello Balsamo, 1999), 129ff.

50. Cf. above, n. 22.

51. Ample bibliography in Lorizio, *Rivelazione*, 131 (122, 123).

52. J.-L. Marion, *Dieu sans l'être* (Paris, 1982); Marion, "Esquisse d'un concept phénoménologique du don," *Archivio di Filosofia* 62 (1994): 75-94.

53. See pp. 58-67 elow.

54. Lorizio, "Attese di salvezza," 31.

The Mythological Conception of Truth   The deficit of an account of truth that marginalizes the intellect's relation to being and is reductively centered on experience resurfaces in pluralistic theology's tendency to content itself with merely historical and phenomenological presentations of religious experience. The problem, in other words, is that of a "mythological" interpretation of truth. This interpretation aims to overcome the idea of truth as "adequation" of man's intelligence to the reality of being and takes its bearings solely from the experience of the subject. It is the subject who is "adequately disposed with respect to the statements" he makes.[55] This concept of truth has become widespread in some currents of the theology of religions; it amounts to a reinterpretation of the language of christological dogma in order to make acceptable Christianity's scandalous claim to uniqueness based on the "truth" of the incarnation. This truth claim is thus reread as "mythological." To be sure, proponents of this view usually begin by affirming that "the 'myth' is not a false language: it belongs, in what concerns its 'truth,' *to the metaphorical-imaginary, poetic sphere.* Such 'truth' however, should remain in the sphere of the myth and should not be confused with the 'literal meaning.'"[56]

To say that the *truth* of the Christian dogma of the incarnation should not be understood as "literal truth" accordingly means that this truth has nothing to do with a "statement of the facts," an "affirmation of objective realities that occurred in history," or "a language of an indicative nature," *but with an expressive language* that "evokes only a subjective attitude": "the assertion and the real value of the doctrine of the incarnation is not of an indicative nature, but rather an *expressive* one: it does not aim to affirm a metaphysical fact, but rather to express an evaluation and to evoke an attitude."[57]

Now the specificity of the truth of Christian language concerning the incarnation lies in its being an "event-person" (John 14:6), an event of the "Word of God" revealed in Jesus of Nazareth, who is "truth" (John 14:6; 17:17b). "Its meaning is ontologically dense."[58] This is true both objectively and subjectively, insofar as the believer's welcoming of the event of truth through the action of the Holy Spirit of truth (John 14:17; 15:26; 16:13) plays

---

55. International Theological Commission, "Il cristianesimo e le religioni," 14.

56. J. Hick, ed., *The Myth of God Incarnate* (London, 1977).

57. J. Hick, "Jesus and the World Religions," in Hick, *The Myth of God Incarnate*, 177f.

58. R. Schnackenburg, "Il concetto giovanneo di verità," in Schnackenburg, *Il vangelo di Giovanni*, IV/2 (Brescia, 1977), 362.

an essential part in this truth. By contrast, the "mythical" account of truth dissolves the unity of the event by affirming its truth in a subjective sense only; it is true merely as a linguistic expression of human attitudes and sentiments. Christian language does not reveal *the reality of an event that actually happened — the personal coming of God in Jesus* Christ. It expresses rather a "reality" belonging to the psychological imagination of the religious subject, albeit one that can evoke the same experience in others. The Christian conviction that God is truly in Jesus Christ is not based on "being in itself" or any full revelation of the Trinity. Christian religious experience is not singular and unique. Christians should not only accept the possibility of religious pluralism, but should also affirm the necessity of an interreligious dialogue in which all religions come together as equals without any claim to some singular truth that the others do not possess. All this appears to contrast sharply with contemporary epistemology's much-debated concept of truth.

Christology and Truth

The metaphysical exigency of Truth, which awakens man to "search for truth," already sets him within a religious horizon; one "who seeks the Truth" is *"one who lives by faith."*[59] This reinforces the profound connection between *the truth that enlightens human reason* and *the gift of "truth" that comes from the light of Christ.* As *Fides et Ratio* explains it, this is ultimately because "man's perfection . . . does not lie in the simple acquisition of an abstract knowledge of the truth, but also consists of a living relationship of giving and trusting another. In this faithfulness that knows how to give of itself, man finds full certainty and security. At the same time, however, knowledge by belief, which is based on interpersonal fidelity, is not without reference to the truth: the believing man trusts in the truth that another shows him" (*FR*, 32).

---

59. *FR*, 31: "belief often turns out to be humanly richer than simple evidence, because it includes an interpersonal connection and puts into play not only the personal cognitive capacities, but also the more radical capacity to trust other people, entering into a more stable and intimate connection with them."

Christology in the Horizon of Truth

There are still other problematic approaches to this delicate relationship. First of all, there is the attempt to submit the *veritas Christiana* to a principle of truth governed by a decadent concept of the rationality of truth. *Not every concept of reason validly mediates reason's encounter with Christian truth.*[60] At certain periods in Christian history a predominant ontology has decentered theology from the revelation of the triune God in Jesus Christ, the fulfillment of the revelation of truth, and has instead submitted the intelligence of the faith to a pre-Christian, if not anti-Christian, concept of truth.[61] In this sense Andrea Milano seems to be correct when he observes that Christian theology too often based itself on assumptions that, while appearing to be rational and, therefore, intrinsically valid, were essentially pre-Christian or, at the very least, not sifted christologically. Again and again theologians have taken over decisive concepts such as being, one, good, infinite, spirit, transcendental, value, history, liberation, and indeed truth — without testing them methodically against a criterion formed by revelation in Jesus Christ.[62]

On the other hand, the dogmatic refusal of any metaphysics, as if it could be nothing but rationalism or a hangover from scholasticism, has pushed theology back into a fideism that "fails to recognize the importance of rational knowledge and philosophical discourse for the understanding of faith, indeed for the very possibility of belief in God" (*FR,*

---

60. In modern culture reason has thus ceased to play the role of "universal wisdom": "it has been gradually reduced to one of the many fields of human knowing; indeed in some ways it has been consigned to a wholly marginal role. Other forms of rationality have acquired an ever higher profile, making philosophical learning appear all the more peripheral. These forms of rationality are directed not towards the contemplation of truth and the search for the ultimate goal and meaning of life; but instead, as 'instrumental reason,' they are directed — actually or potentially — towards the promotion of utilitarian ends, towards enjoyment or power" (*FR,* 47).

61. See the illuminating essays of Andrea Milano on this aspect: "'Analogia Christi'. Il parlare intorno a Dio in una teologia cristiana," *Ricerche Teologiche* 1 (1990): 29-73; "Aletheia. La 'concentrazione cristologica' della verità," *Filosofia e Teologie* 4 (1990): 13-45; "Padre," *Filosofia e Teologie* 5 (1991): 445-62; "Teodicea e Cristologia," *Filosofia e Teologie* 7 (1993): 276-300. See also L. Saccone, "Sulla concentrazione cristologica della verità," in A. Ascione and P. Guistiniani, *Il Cristo. Nuovo criterio in filosofia e teologia?* (Naples, 1995), 85-110; A. Milano, *Quale Verità. Per una critica della ragione teologica* (Bologna, 1999).

62. Milano, *Quale Verità,* 13.

59

55).[63] Now a correct reciprocal relationship between reason's need for metaphysical truth and the light derived from "revelation" requires a mutual interpenetration of faith and reason (36ff.) that avoids the drama of their separation (4-49). This requires, in turn, a concept of "human reason" open to the absolute aspect of the truth. The concrete man who knows, speaks, and acts must be able to perceive *the anticipation of something ultimate, unconditioned, and absolute* precisely within his historical situation. In every search for truth, even in the particular and the finite, man always supposes an absolute truth that allows him to judge the particular and finite as such. A *light of truth always precedes us and presents itself to our intelligence.*

The recognition of the undeniable historical and cultural conditioning of our knowledge does not ipso facto warrant any form of relativism, skepticism, or perspectivism, since "philosophy itself suggests that *historically conditioned and restricted statements nonetheless contain something like an anticipation of the whole and therefore of what is permanently valid and unconditioned.* In the life of every man there are fundamental and ultimate choices towards which his action is directed."[64] There is, then, a *dogmatic structure of intelligence* that enlightens and guides every cognitive act in its own particular historical and cultural determination; this structure does not impede but rather allows man to recognize and grasp, precisely by way of its inner movement, "universal truths."

Human reason, then, has a value based on the knowledge of a single, universal, and always valid truth. But if theology must presuppose that human intelligence has this fundamental dogmatic structure, it must not ignore the historical need to interpret individual statements of truth conditioned by history and time. Theology must not forget, in other words, the fundamental critical problem of the relation between ever valid "universal truth" and the "historicity" of human thought itself *(the problem of hermeneutics and metaphysics).*

This conception of reason in terms of truth can mediate between hermeneutics and metaphysics. But it requires going back to the foundation

---

63. "One currently widespread symptom of this fideistic tendency is a 'biblicism' which tends to make the reading and exegesis of Sacred Scripture the sole criterion of truth. In consequence, the word of God is identified with Sacred Scripture alone, thus eliminating the doctrine of the Church which the Second Vatican Council stressed quite specifically" (*FR*, 55).

64. W. Kasper, "Riproposizione del principio dogmatico," in Kasper, *Teologia e Chiesa* (Brescia, 1989), 35, italics mine.

of the *metaphysical and epistemological primacy of being,* that is, to the *original metaphysical experience of being.* This experience lays the foundation of thought itself and attests to the "presence" of "truth" in thought. This essential "relation to being" is constitutive of thought. It has two functions, both of which need to be respected if theology is to be a critical *intellectus fidei.* First, intelligence opens to the "truth of being" through an intuitive "intellection." Second, it opens to the "truth of being" in a speculative, analytical, discursive way as "reason"; by means of this second function it attains through judgment to the "truth of the thing" by establishing its "adequation" to the being grasped in the first function.

The Horizon of the Truth of Being   The *first aspect* of human knowing is "intellection." This intellection is the *primum,* the primary *metaphysical intuition that coexists with thought itself and is its foundation.* Intellect *is* intellective thought *insofar as its action attests to the presence of the truth of being.* We touch here the essence of thought itself: to think is to think *being as reality* that lights up and becomes manifest *(alétheia)* in thought. The *critical realism of thought,* as intellective intuition, is especially necessary in order to respond to our current crisis of speculative reason; *it reminds us that intelligence is not dominated by conceptual abstraction alone,* but is first of all a faculty for the concrete, *for being as the act that makes all things exist.*[65] Metaphysical experience cannot be reduced to a concept but is rather the intuition of the indefinable presence of being as act, thanks to which the objects of thought (concrete beings) light up in consciousness. *It is not so much a content of thought as an inexhaustible container.* It is in the light of being that we intuit and judge all things.[66]

Intellective knowing is, in the last analysis, submission to being, *assent to a truth of thought that consists in acknowledging, and conforming to, the reality of being.* Clearly, this account of truth does not oppose "unveiling" and "correspondence," but rather integrates them. Being reveals itself

65. B. Rioux, *L'être et la vérité chez Heidegger et Saint Thomas d'Aquin* (Montréal and Paris, 1963), 185-86.

66. Rioux, 182f. In order to illustrate this intuitive capacity of knowing that is based on an immediate and ineffable encounter with the event of the self-manifestation of the reality of the concrete (the event of the unconcealment of the concrete), the reader can usefully consider Heidegger's remarks on art: in the understanding of a work of art, thought does not proceed from the concept of the work, but from the work toward the horizon of its understanding. See M. Heidegger, *Sentieri interrotti* (Florence, 1968), 21.

(alétheia); it is borne upon the mind, which intuits being and, in the act of judgment, acknowledges its conformity to being, "recognizing" the ontological mystery of being's presence in the concrete things upon which it bestows existence. Knowledge is thus *the core of an intellective welcoming that venerates the "mystery" of being, acknowledges it, heeds its call, and accepts it with gratitude.*[67] It is a knowledge that does not dominate, but loves, adores, and lets be. *Truth, then, does not arise because of the questions that I have posed according to my categories.* Rather, it is the truth that presents itself, reshaping my categories and commanding my attention. The mind does not develop a "useful truth," but cares for and respects "the truth" in itself, which alone *gives existence meaning and light.*

As I have mentioned, the *horizon* of man's search for truth makes sense of two important affirmations. First, man's search leads him to *religion:* "the search for the truth is a first *vocatio ad credendum.*" "The man who seeks the truth is also one who lives by faith" (*FR,* 31). Second, the search for truth, as a response to this vocation, recalls *our need for the other as a companion on the path to truth* (the dialogical principle: *FR,* 33). *The principle that religious truth is dialogical can thus bring together not only those who explicitly reside within the "Christian" horizon of truth,* in which the experience of truth is fulfilled in communion and growth, but also all human beings who explicitly or implicitly *set out on an authentic and sincere search for the truth* in an attitude of acceptance of, and listening to, the truth.

Christology in the Horizon of the Metaphysical Experience of Being   This horizon of thought is extremely important for Christology. This is especially true insofar as Christology is fundamentally and necessarily an attempt to understand the proclamation *of the event of the Word as it gives itself in history.* This attempt to understand the mystery is just that, a humble and *contemplative* opening to the singularity and ineffability of the event of revealed truth. It recalls the primary form of *thinking,* which is particularly consistent with *faith: welcoming of the truth of the event of Christ through listening.* This experiential contact and encounter with the Word of truth grounds and gives meaning to its interpretation. Faith's "contemplative" reflection on the event of truth that reveals itself and carries the principles of its own interpretation retrieves a sense of the *intellectus fidei*

---

67. P. Gilbert, *La semplicità del principio. Introduzione alla metafisica* (Casale Monferrato, 1992), 318f.

that is more *experiential,* more *sapiential,* and more connected to the *narrative* structure[68] of the event of truth. Graced understanding thus bursts forth as a light from within the narration that attests that the revealed truth opens its own way to man (John 14:6).[69] The Christology of the Fathers and monastic writers is recovered in this theology, which better reflects the concept of truth revealed in the foundational event of Christ.

On the other hand, this encounter with the truth given historically in Jesus Christ displays the personal character of specifically Christian truth (the *persona veritatis*). I have already noted that dialogical relationality points to a personal conception of that truth. Man's aspiration to truth leads to a truth that is concretized in a personal absolute — an absolute person — who manifests himself to man in a real "self-gift" in history *(truth as event).* It follows that interpersonal relation calls human freedom into play on the journey toward a personal truth. Love, then, is decisive both for the access to truth (epistemology) and for the intrinsic content of the truth itself (ontology of love). Indeed, "[h]uman perfection . . . consists not simply in acquiring an abstract knowledge of the truth, but in a dynamic relationship of faithful self-giving with others. It is in this faithful self-giving that a person finds a fullness of certainty and security. At the same time, however, knowledge through belief, grounded as it is on trust between persons, is linked to truth: in the act of believing, men and women entrust themselves to the truth which the other declares to them" (*FR*, 32).

68. "It would be naïve as well as erroneous to oppose narrative and theological reason." B. Sesboüé, "Récit et raison théologique," in Sesboüé, *Jésus-Christ l'unique médiateur. II. Les récits du salut* (Paris, 1991), 31f. Sesboüé refers to P. Corset's essay, "Le théologien face au conteur évangélique. la recherche d'une théologie narrative," *Recherches de Science Religieuse* 73 (1985): 74-78.

69. "Truth *gives* itself to be known through the piercing word of its appearing. It cannot be grasped. It can only be introduced — in being seen and heard — into the intimacy of knowledge. The word or miracle of truth expands in us to the point of being the space in which we love: we begin to 'dwell' in the Word and the Word in us" (H. Schlier, "Meditazioni sul concetto giovanneo di verità," in Schlier, *Riflessioni sul Nuovo Testamento* [Brescia, 1969], 357).

Marcello Bordoni

Truth in a Christological Horizon

In the perspective outlined above, truth is at once a welcoming of, and a response to, the personal event of truth in Jesus Christ. This event finds its center in the incarnation and the paschal mystery. It achieves the eschatological revelation of the Trinity and is the fundamental rule of theological truth. Theological knowledge cannot deviate from this christological concentration without losing its identity. This knowledge presupposes that intelligence is an opening to truth, but it is governed by the event of the personal truth manifested in history — in the incarnation and paschal mystery. It must be measured by the veiling and unveiling of this christological event. This theological knowing establishes a primary conception of theology as *critical knowledge of faith.* This model of theology privileges the apprehension and reception of the event of revealed truth. Christology is the horizon and the content of the truth of the Christian faith.

Truth as Doxology   The christocentric model of theology suggests that to judge is to acknowledge the truth itself on the basis not only of logical affirmation, but also of loving decision. It is a doing of theology that not only presupposes but also unfolds within the movement of faith that thanks, loves, and hopes for the perfect encounter with the whole truth that is Christ.[70] It could be defined as an "intellectual contemplation within the mystery of salvation," or else as "a journey of the spiritual soul towards the light of truth that redeems and beatifies, yet which does not exclude polemic, apologetic, and the labor of the concept."[71] There is greater freedom for creativity, inspiration, and symbolic or narrative lan-

---

70. We could call this style of theology "doxological," inasmuch as it gives a "eucharistic" cast to the very structure of theological discourse. If it is to define itself as thought within the very act of faith, this style or model of theology must do its reflection in accord with the spiritual movement of a knowing that is acknowledgment, re-cognition. In this movement, in fact, man finds completion precisely by letting God, or God's Word, speak and think him. See Bordoni, "Riflessioni introduttive," 27-28.

71. The specific mark of this theology may be characterized in the following way. It is a real reflection on faith, but it is not "rational": "It is *sapiential* . . . not rational or scientific. It is speculative and systematic in its own way, but its object is the intelligible certitude of spiritual vision, not the rational certification of discursive thought" (M. Seckler, *Teologia Scienza Chiesa. Saggi di teologia fondamentale* [Brescia, 1988], 34).

guage; the objective is more discovery than foundational argumentation; it is closer to prayer, meditation, and preaching. To the man who is sincerely searching for the truth and for a Person in whom to trust, the Christian faith holds out the truth personified in Jesus Christ ("the truth which is in Jesus Christ": Eph. 4:21; Col. 1:15-20). Christ "is" the "truth" (John 14:6) of God, the eternal Word, precisely as *incarnate;* his entire person reveals the Father (*DV,* 4). The truth, therefore, which man's mind and heart seek, without being able to know its personal face ("the unknown God": Acts 17:23), can be reached only through Jesus Christ, the fullness of the truth.[72]

Christological Truth in Argumentative Theology What I have said should not lead us to neglect the reflexive, argumentative, and systematic aspect of human thought. This aspect cannot be isolated from the first, nor considered secondary to reason's epistemological process. Today's crisis of reason threatens to plunge this aspect into oblivion.[73] It thus also threatens the acceptance of the truth that reveals and gives itself in being.[74] For being does not present itself to our intelligence as a perceptible object in its own right, but in our encounter with particular facts, persons, and things in which its light shines.[75] Now in the knowledge of sensible, particular things, in the encounter with persons, in concrete events, in the knowledge of entities in general, reason, acting in the light of being, performs a series of equally fundamental functions: analysis, abstraction, and

72. G. Lafont, "Verso un rinnovato orientamento eucaristico del linguaggio teologico," in *Il sapere teologico e il suo metodo,* 257-70.

73. "The human disappointment of a type of thought centered on entities in forgetfulness of being re-opens the 'problem of being,' but, it seems, in a way that is still forgetful of being" (G. Lafont, *Dio, il Tempo e l'Essere* [Casale Monferrato, 1992], 191, 222-23).

74. In Thomistic epistemology, simple apprehension is aligned with the essence of the thing, while judgment pertains to being itself. This does not mean, however, that the prepredicative aspect is a mere logical operation that produces concepts separated from real existence. It is rather reality itself, the given as such, that we know as both intelligible and sensible. Apprehension is not blind to existence. Rather, it grasps essence (in the concept) as a *modus essendi,* a "certain mode of exercising the act of existence." In the very act of forming concepts, the understanding sees the ontological data of essence in relation to being. For the main Thomistic loci on this point, see Rioux, 169-85.

75. Thus, while it is true that human understanding rests upon the metaphysical experience of being, this light does not shine except in the perception of entities known through the senses. See Gilbert, 293-321.

deduction on the one hand, judgment, argument, and truth declaration on the other.[76] In this unavoidable duty of reason, theology finds a new horizon of truth in that person who is truth and in the historical event of the incarnation, cross, and resurrection. It is within this horizon that it understands every particular dogmatic statement. Just as speculative reason perceives the entity in its "judgment," understanding it formally in the light of being, in its essential relationship to the "truth," theological reason, measured by the event of Christ, "understands" every dogmatic statement in the light of him who says "I am the truth" (John 14:6). It is thus that every particular "object" of Christian thought *is understood as God's "truth" in its indissoluble relationship to the incarnate person of Jesus Christ crucified and risen.*

This second aspect of "theological reason" is also fundamental for the believer's access to the *event of truth in the Christian faith.* In this perspective "Christology," the rule of Christian thought, *reshapes the proclamation of faith,* translating the history of salvation in which the Word of God is made manifest into a coherent system of truth, "moving from a 'narrative of the things that have been accomplished among us just as they were delivered to us by those who from the beginning were eyewitnesses and ministers of the Word' (Lk 1:1-2) to a speculative account where concepts and propositions follow one another in a logical order thanks to a marvelous harmony inscribed in the nature of things."[77] Certainly this passage from the "historical form of revelation" to the "systematic form of the theological treatise" raises questions, especially today: *Is it legitimate to separate* the *content* from the *historical form* of divine revelation? The latter is centered on a *singular and unrepeatable* event: "the christological event," the coming of the *persona veritatis,* which takes place at a particular place and time. The principle of "truth as adequation," on the other hand, privileges explanation and norm, in other words, what has a universal value *semper et ubique.*

The history recounted in the Scriptures finds in the speculative system the proof, so to speak, of its perennial and universal truth. While the sacred story reveals the plot of the divine design through signs and fig-

---

76. For a detailed analysis of these functions, see Bordoni, "Il problem della struttura del sapere teologico," in *Il sapere teologico e il suo metodo,* 25-34.

77. E. Benvenuto, "Attuali statuti epistemologici e filosofici della verità," *Rassegna Teologica* 29 (1988): 45.

ures, whose ultimate fulfillment is the christological event, theological system tends to develop the *how and why,* the ultimate foundation of the narrative discourse. But this second aspect of the work of reason in theology is important *not only because of the nature of rationality,* which faith does not reject, but also because of the supernatural enlightenment of reason, that is, *because of the structure of faith itself,* which always combines the narrating of the salvific events with the elaboration of categories, concepts, interpretations in a specifically doctrinal framework. This body of doctrine, however, must never be made independent of the narrative.[78]

Christology as the Revealed Fulfillment of Truth

Christology presupposes "the horizon of the truth" that defines man's orientation toward the "mystery of transcendence" and *places him, at the same time, in an attitude of seeking and expectation.* At the same time, what we have said suggests that in announcing the christological event as an "event of truth," Christology gives to human seeking and expectation its definitive response. Hence the indispensable importance of the "dialogue" with philosophy, the human sciences, and the world religions. Christology cannot exempt itself from this dialogue; yet this dialogue must always be normed by truth and must culminate decisively in the announcement of Christ as truth. X. Tilliette rightly observes that *"fides quaerens intellectum* is not exclusively theological, but also philosophical, that is, faith seeks not only to get clear about itself (in theology), but enlightens philosophy, the exercise of so-called natural reason, and promotes its development."[79]

---

78. Sesboüé, 31. P. Beauchamp, *Le récit, la lettre et le corps. Essais bibliques* (Paris, 1982), 191-92, shows the *solidarity in the Bible between narrative and law.* Far from being mutually exclusive, narrative and norm are complementary, indeed, imply each other. The narrative of the institution of the Jewish Passover is a privileged example of this claim. We could transpose this structure — narrative and norm — into the terms of "narrative" and "dogma," inasmuch as dogma expresses the binding character of the content of faith.

79. X. Tilliette, *Le vicende della "filosofia cristiana" nell'800 alla luce del dibattito del 900,* cited in G. Lorizio, *Rassegna Teologica* 30 (1989): 558.

Jesus Christ: The Personal Event of Truth

Christian thought, then, must take note of the importance, which is both singular and universal, of the christological statement of John 14:6 ("I am the truth")[80] for faith and for reason. This assertion sums up the whole christological and theological meaning of Christian revelation; understood correctly, it allows us to grasp the essential reasons for the singularity and universality of its claim to truth.

In order to interpret John 14:6 correctly, we need to see it in light of the economy of salvation. Jesus' words "and you know where I am going" (14:4) prompt Thomas's question: "how can we know the way?" (14:5b).[81] Thomas's question provokes Jesus to go beyond his own question (14:6). In his response Jesus proclaims himself the "way" *(hodós)* before calling himself "the truth" *(alétheia)* and "the life" *(zoé)*. In a certain sense the term "way" is most important here, because it "formally expresses the mediation of Jesus and describes in a kind of synthesis the essence of the work of salvation, which consists in making us participants in the life of the Father."[82] Still, the soteriological force of the statement "I am the way" surpasses the question. Jesus' statement does not mean, in fact, that he is "a way" toward the truth.[83] It means rather that he *is the way to the Father because he is the truth and the life.* Unlike pagan gnosticism and especially hermeticism, John sees the "truth" as the reason why Jesus *is the way itself* in a completely singular and unique manner. The economic sense in which Jesus is "the only way" to the Father ("no one comes to the Father but by me": 14:6b) reveals *the theological-trinitarian reason for this singular statement: Jesus is the truth of the Father, in person, who therefore gives eternal life[84] and is the only way which leads to him.* This personalization of Jesus being the "way, the

80. I. de la Potterie, "Io sono la via, la verità, e la vita," in *Studi di cristologia giovannea* (Genoa, 1986), 124-54.

81. See A. Milano, "Alétheia. La concentrazione cristologica della verità," in Milano, *Quale Verità,* 91-156, for bibliography on this point.

82. De la Potterie, 150.

83. As is well known, this seems to have been the exegesis of Augustine and Aquinas, for whom truth and life appear to be at the end of the way, that is, in the Word, in God (see de la Potterie, 126; Milano, *Quale verità,* 98-130).

84. The juxtaposition of the terms "truth" and "life" in a soteriological context suggests that Jesus bestows the *life of the Father* precisely by means of the gift of truth.

truth, the life" rules out any *purely phenomenological and functionalist* interpretation of Christ's extraordinary claim to be the "truth." Jesus is thus not only "the truth relative to men," as if he had made known to us nothing about his person. Jesus is not only a revealer or preacher of truth like the ancient prophets or the apostles who were only instruments of revelation. None of them ever claimed to be the truth. *Jesus is the only way because he is identical with the truth itself and is thus the very fullness of revelation.* He is, in his person, the total and definitive revelation of the Father par excellence.

The first quality, therefore, that stands out in Christ's claim to be the *persona veritatis*[85] places us before an entirely new fact: the fundamental epistemological question of Christology is not "*what* is the truth?" but rather "*who* is the truth?" To be sure, this statement cannot remain closed in a static ontology, separated both from the dynamic of the trinitarian horizon and from the historical dynamic of the revelatory event of the incarnation of the eternal Word.

The Trinitarian Significance of Christ's Being the Truth in Person

In reality the *person of Christ,* who proclaims himself "truth" (an assertion inseparable from the incarnation) and is therefore the life and way for man, cannot be understood apart from the *trinitarian relations.* Jesus Christ's being "truth," which occupies a central place between the "way" and the "life," is thus essentially a matter of his relation to the Father, from whom he "comes" toward man and to whom he is "turned" (John 14:2-4) as the only way.[86] For this reason "no one comes to the Father but by me" (14:6), and only by knowing him is it possible to know the Father (14:7). While the term "way" is the *key word* in this passage of John, it is also true that his being the (only) "way"[87] depends on his being the truth in person. This "being truth" is defined, again, in relation to the Father, "with whom" he is one ("he who has seen me has seen the Father": 14:9) in a reciprocal

85. Milano, "'Analogia Christi,'" 29.
86. M. Bordoni, "Gesù Cristo, Via unica del Padre verso l'uomo," in Bordoni, "L'esperienza di Gesù e le fede dogmatica di Calcedonia," in *Lat* 65 (1999): 510ff.
87. The peremptory statement: "no one" comes to the Father but by me (14:6b).

relation (14:10-11). Therefore Jesus is not a "transitory," "temporary," or "contingent" way through which the believer must pass in order to reach the Father, leaving the way behind and immersing himself "in the indeterminate abyss of divinity."[88]

On the other hand, this trinitarian context, while defining the primary sense in which Christ is the truth in person, cannot be separated from the event of the incarnation and paschal mystery. Christ's identity with truth is rooted in his being the Son and eternal Word of the Father who contains the paternal wisdom. Nevertheless, he is truth particularly in the history of his coming from the Father, whereby he becomes the revealer par excellence, revealing and communicating his truth to men. The key to his being truth is thus his "turning toward" the Father — a turning that gives the entire history of the incarnation a paschal connotation (16:28). Christ's earthly existence culminates in the cross and resurrection, the event that fulfills the supreme meaning of his being the truth. The resurrection is the supreme hour of the revelation of the Trinity through "the Only-begotten Son turned to the bosom of the Father."[89] The trinitarian being of the Son, in his relationship with the Father, finds its immanent expression in the very mystery of God. The Son is the Word (1:1-2). But this Word becomes truth for men only to the extent that it is revealed to them.[90] At the same time, insofar as the incarnation is revelation, it manifests to us the one who is the truth in himself, that is, the eternal Word of the Father.

The Essential Dimensions of the Incarnate, Personal Truth

The immanent Trinity, in its totally gratuitous manifestation in history, in its free will to reveal, calls human beings by means of an equally free en-

---

88. M. Eckhart speaks of this abyss as "a darkness in which the light of the Trinity never shines": conclusion to *Sermo 'Ave gratia plena'* (J. Quint, ed., *Deutsche Predigten und Traktate* [Hanser, 1955], 261).

89. I prefer this translation, which brings out the way in which the Son is turned toward the bosom of the Father. This turning expresses not only the directionality of the Son within the Trinity, but also the unveiling of this Son through the return of the Risen One to the Father.

90. De la Potterie, 152.

counter, in the interpersonal answer of faith, with this truth-as-freedom manifested once and for all in Christ. The intrinsic call of truth in conscience and reason implicitly contains the proposal of the Father's plan to manifest himself in Christ the truth. Thus "the retrieval of truth as event permits Christian thought to gain the simplicity of a single perspective. Such a religious outlook makes perceptible the unity between the *absolute* and the historical, the *necessary* and the *free* as a primary evidence without diminishing the import of the distinctions that the West has articulated in the course of its cultural development."[91]

The truth *(alétheia)* that is Christ, as a personal event, therefore implies a manifold movement that gives it a complex content.

1. In the Christian view Christ's truth, which cannot be understood without the event of the incarnation, and life is not a matter of the divinity, as if his being the way were tied exclusively to his humanity. "Jesus Christ is entirely truth in the totality of his person, but insofar as it is unfolded historically in his words and deeds *invicem inter se connexis* (see *DV,* 2)."[92] Now this event of truth moves in two directions at once. The first, descending direction is the Word of truth's coming from the Father. In the second, ascending direction, this same incarnate Word returns to the Father (John 1:18; 7:29-33; 13:3; 16:28). This means that the event of the truth gets its epistemological shape from the saving revelation that happened in history — from the event that visibly, in the realism of Christ's fleshliness

---

91. Scola, "I principi del dialogo interreligioso," 214; Scola, "Libertà umana e verità a partire dall'Enciclica *Fides et Ratio,*" in *Il risveglio della ragione, proposte per un pensiero credente,* 85-111.

92. Saccone, 105; Milano, *Quale Verità,* 138. The incarnation is indeed the definitive event of the economy of revelation. This economy, after all, takes the form of a descent of the eternal Word in which Christ, the truth, reveals to us the secrets of the Father (John 1:18). From this fundamental point of view we can say that Christ the revealer opens the "way of truth" to us, and in this descent founds, through his incarnation, the truth of human language (which consists of words and deeds); of his own historical human reality; of his authentic knowledge, consciousness, and experience of his identity as Son and of his relation to the Father; and of the revelatory language in which he speaks to us in truth of the Father and of man *(analogia Christi).* Christ's speech, then, is neither purely symbolic nor radically apophatic. Christ's being man is essentially symbolic (sacramental), thanks to the incarnation, of the eternal Word; his human experience and language are able to go infinitely beyond the range of purely human language, which is founded only on the "creaturely analogy" of being. Christ's experience and language become a revelation, a sacrament, of the new creation, which, of course, takes root in man's openness to the knowledge of the truth.

(1 John 4:2-3), reveals to us the twofold trinitarian movement of the eternal Word who, in the bosom of the Father, is begotten by him and turns back toward him.

2. By reason of this twofold aspect of the dynamic event of the incarnation, Christ the truth can be called the way in person. He is such not only by reason of the humanity he assumed, as if his humanity were merely the way to the divinity (as in the Augustinian and Thomistic exegesis of this passage). Christ is the only way to the Father primarily because he is the Word who comes down to our humanity at the Father's bidding. Christianity joins two movements that the other religions tend to separate. These religions are dominated by the movement of ascent.[93] In Christianity, on the other hand, everything depends on God's descent.[94] In contrast to certain tendencies in non-Christian mysticism, faith in Christ proclaims the unfathomable depths of love that allow God to be encountered in creation and in the "limitations" of man's poverty. "Other religions know that God is rich in heaven. That he wanted to be poor alongside his creatures, even suffer, and, through the incarnation, show creatures this pain of his love: this is the absolute novelty that Christ brought."[95]

While the movement of the way of truth comes from above, faith in Christ includes, thanks to the incarnation, a movement from below: from the incarnate Son toward the Father. By his descent toward man (revelation), the eternal Word who becomes the truth opens up the way *to* the Father. This way, which does not exclude his humanity, is the only way to the Father because it is the way that the Father himself has opened by sending his Son to us. True, Christ's being the only way to the Father is not based theologically on the existence of his humanity as such, but on his physiognomy as the incarnate Son and Logos in person. Nevertheless, it is in his humanity that he manifests the essential movement of trinitarian convergence toward the Father, and it is through his humanity, crucified and risen, that he invites man to travel the way to the Father. Hence the impor-

93. G. Marchesi, *La Cristologia di H. U. v. Balthasar. La figura di Gesù Cristo espressione visibile di Dio* (Rome, 1977), 161; Marchesi, *La cristologia trinitaria di Hans Urs von Balthasar* (Brescia, 1997).

94. M. Jöri, *Descensus Dei. Teologia della croce nell'opera di H. U. v. Balthasar* (Rome, 1981).

95. K. Lehmann and W. Kasper, *Hans Urs von Balthasar. Figura ed opera* (Casale Monferrato, 1991), 12-13.

tance of the Augustinian and Thomistic idea that Jesus' humanity is the way as a convergence upon the Father.

> It is crucial to see, however, that Christ's being the way to the Father passes through the personalization in the Word and Son of the human in the integrity of its complex, corporeal-spiritual, exterior and experiential nature. Thus, he is not only the fullness of God's revelation to man, but also the perfect model of the attitude of obedience and abandonment in accord with the Father's will, which is his universal plan to save all human beings. He who is the only way because he is the truth and the life descends to man and is thus also the way that invites all men to ascend to the Father, to invoke him in a communion of prayer, in perfect obedience to the divine will.[96]

The task is thus to define the order between the two movements; they are not successive, but rather simultaneous, and together they constitute the single dynamism of the event of "christological truth." We thus glimpse *the profound connection between the "mystery of the truth" which shines as the light of the being, as a source of intelligibility in human knowledge, and the "truth of God's self-communication of self in Jesus Christ."* The "logos of revelation," achieved in the event of Jesus Christ the truth, is not faith's only source of intelligibility, as if we could and should cast away, root and branch, any positive contribution of human reason. The intelligence of faith does not come from faith alone; it is not only the reason of faith. As Emilio Brito points out,

> every revelation of God is mediated by being as being. . . . For this reason, the original word that flows from being is also the *medium* of divine Revelation. And the interpretation of the word and the event of Revelation — that is, theological thought — has always been worked out in the *medium* of philosophical thought. The event of Revelation therefore does not take place "alongside" being, as if it were something

---

96. Bordoni, "L'esperienza di Gesù e la fede dogmatica di Calcedonia," 513. What we have just said should not be taken as suggesting that Jesus' being the way to the Father in his historical humanity is simply an example, an ethical model to be imitated in (perfect) obedience and offering. At the basis of every moral imitation is a real communion that, through faith and the sacraments of faith, makes effective — through him, with him, and in him (eucharistic liturgy) — the passage (Passover) to the Father on that way to the Father that he, Jesus, himself is.

added from the outside. . . . . Even though it is supernatural, Revelation occurs in the *heart of being itself*: it reveals the ultimate depths of being and illuminates it from its own transcendence.[97]

Reflection on being, in the logos of revelation, should therefore not be considered merely a provisional phase from which theological thought would finally free itself in order to attain a God "without being" by passing from the logos-word toward the infinite spaces of an eternal silence. Far from being suppressed, the light of being continues to shine in the light of the mystery;[98] we must therefore conceive the manifestation of being and the event of the revelation of the "truth" carried out in Christ as a unity. This unity does not, of course, abolish their every difference. If a "pure" revelation were to take place in itself alone, outside of the light of being, would it not be entirely "unthinkable"? Would not the very possibility of a theology itself be radically nullified? On the other hand, *the thought of the being is confirmed by the event of revelation,* even as it comes from this profoundly historical event that is open to new perspectives originating from divine truth.[99]

What I have said up until now concerning the "christological concentration of the truth" calls for the complement of the pneumatological aspect, with which I will deal in a later study.

---

97. E. Brito, *Dieu et l'être d'après Thomas d'Aquin et Hegel* (Paris, 1991), 22.

98. G. Siewerth, *Das Schicksal der Metaphysik von Thomas zu Heidegger* (Einsiedeln, 1959), 511.

99. Siewerth, 27, 80, 516; Brito, 22.

Theologies of Religious Pluralism

MASSIMO SERRETTI

Many of the exponents of the theory of religious pluralism base their case on an observation on which they expect there to be general agreement: the isolation of the world's religions, each within its own cultural and territorial limits, is over, and the religions now find themselves in a more or less close, more or less challenging coexistence. This observation is usually accompanied by another, which is roughly as follows. World peace, it is said, is a necessity. But history teaches us that political entities cannot peacefully coexist unless there is a certain level of mutual understanding among different religious affiliations. Dialogue, mutual recognition, and coexistence are thus a *conditio sine qua non* of world peace. Interreligious theory and practice, combined with an ethic of liberation on behalf of all who suffer, will bring unity and peace to mankind, countering intolerance, fundamentalism, and the exclusivist or inclusivist absolutization of one's own position that either ignores or is hostile to others.

In short, proponents of pluralist theology begin with historical circumstances and end with supposedly binding ethical imperatives. They begin with a philosophy of history and end with a global ethics, believing they can capture the reality of the religions between these two pincers.[1]

---

1. A critique and an alternative proposal can be found in G. Neuhaus, *Kein Welfrieden ohne christlichen Absolutheitsanspruch. Eine religionstheologische Auseinendersetzung mit Hans Küngs "Projekt Weltethos"* (Freiburg, 1999).

This method is, in our judgment, radically unsound.

The pluralistic theology of religions attempts to understand man's religiosity and the historical variety of religions in an account that is more or less indebted to a philosophy of religion and is located somewhere between a philosophy of history and a political ethic. In doing so it sets aside some fundamental facts of anthropology, indeed, of creaturely existence. Such an attempt appears doomed to fail on account of its own acknowledged and unacknowledged premises. Controversy about how to understand religious pluralism is always also controversy about how to interpret human nature and about how realistic revelation may be said to be.[2]

The reduction of fundamental anthropology to the philosophy of religion[3] leads inevitably to the call either for a corrective or for an integration, which, in various leaders of the pluralist theology, takes the form of a more or less voluntaristic philosophy of praxis and a (derivative) theology of social liberation.

The deficiency affecting the systems of John Hick, Paul Knitter, Jacques Dupuis, Raimundo Pannikar, Samartha, and a good number of their pupils and teachers is anthropological before it is christological — even though this christological deficiency cannot be reduced to a merely anthropological one. We have here an analogue to the fallout of the so-called wars of religion in European thought: the formulation of a new notion of "universality"[4] to replace the earlier, supposedly failed account.[5]

---

2. Vatican II's *Nostra Aetate* has brought a decisive clarification on this point. The basic approach of this document serves as a methodological criterion in Gerhard Ludwig Müller's "Ist die Einzigkeit Jesu Christi im Kontext einer pluralistischen Weltzivilisation vermittelbar?" in R. Schwager, *Relativierung der Wahrheit? Kontextuelle Christologie auf dem Prüfstand* (Freiburg, 1998), 169.

3. The explicit premises of this reduction can be found, for example, in *De Veritate* (London, 1645) of Lord Herbert of Cherbury and in other authors such as W. Wollaston. The first step in this reduction was to identify *religio* with *religio naturalis;* the second confined the *religio naturalis* to an operation of discursive reason; the third identified reason as the distinctive trait of man as such. This three-step reduction enabled a reconciliation of religion and of humanism that retained the emancipatory thrust of the Reformation, but without its antihumanistic pessimism.

4. The essential idea is that we are in a new historical situation that calls for a new self-consciousness by human beings, of which the pluralistic theology of religions would be the most appropriate and up-to-date form. This is brought out nicely in H. R. Schlette, "Zur Theologie der Religionen," *Orientierungen* 51 (1987): 156.

5. See the work of Grotius, Pufendorf, Leibniz, and the Abbé de Saint-Pierre.

The project of constructing a "universal peace" required as broad as possible a basis of agreement that transcended the particularity of confessional allegiances, which had shown themselves to be the source of interminable conflicts. A religion that had spawned war could not serve as the foundation of peace. It was therefore necessary to contrive a suprareligious, indeed, a suprahumanistic basis for unity. The crisis of the Renaissance had undermined the humanist faith. The Reformation played a significant role in this process. So, too, did the revival of strongly skeptical and systematically critical currents that prepared the paths later beaten by the Enlightenment, which believed more in the critical power of reason than in the dignity of man. Nevertheless, the turmoil of that age affected what was still a largely Christian, albeit confessionally divided, Europe. The question we must face today on account of the increasing proximity of peoples, cultures, and religions had not yet arisen. That having been said, there remains a considerable affinity between the European thought of the seventeenth century[6] and that of the North American pluralists of the twentieth.

The most striking thing about the pluralists, then, is their failure to structure their proposal around the nature and mystery of the human being. The problems bound up with an account of religion lacking a solid anthropology are equally in evidence. Once we have grasped this, it becomes immediately clear that the pluralists' inattention to the human *physis* entails a failure to give due place and profile to metaphysics or, as Henrici puts it, metaanthropology.[7] In essence, Hick and Knitter are proposing a theology that prescinds from metaphysics and revelation, from anthropology and creation. Naturally these theologies contain an implicit or fragmentary anthropology and metaphysics, even though their stated intention is to do without both. The pluralists opt out of dealing explicitly with, say, human nature as a created reality because creation has an uncomfortably Judeo-Christian ring to it. But this option rules out any explicit appeal to metaphysics and thus prevents access to a level of dialogue that while not being directly religious, is present in every religion as well as in its respective theology. The withdrawal from anthropology and meta-

---

6. For a good introduction to the pluralistic theology of religions, see P. Byrne, *Natural Religion and the Nature of Religion: The Legacy of Deism* (London, 1989); P. Harrison, *"Religion" and the Religions in the English Enlightenment* (Cambridge, 1990). Both authors are inheritors of the deistic tradition, even though they correct it on certain points.

7. P. Henrici, "Meta-fisica o meta-antropologia?" in *Metafisica e scienze dell'uomo. Atti del VII Congresso Internazionale Bergamo 4-9. IX. 1980,* vol. 1 (Rome, 1982), 595-606.

physics is already a serious problem for religion. It is absolutely fatal for Christology.

The decision to leave out of account both human nature and what in human nature points beyond it (metaphysics) lends the majority of pluralistic theologies their singularly naive air, even as it gives them freedom to borrow liberally from disparate authors and traditions. A decisive test of our characterization is the place of the transcendental *verum* in the theology of pluralism.[8] A unity of persons, cultures, and traditions that would avoid being understood in a purely "political" or reductively existentialist way is simply inconceivable outside an attempt to clarify the *quaestio de veritate.*

Man and Truth

Every pluralistic theology of religions must face the question of the one and the many as it bears on the plurality of persons, cultures, and religions. Every such theology is forced by its subject matter to engage the relationship of the one and of the many and to explain the character of this relation in one way or another. This is an inevitability for pluralist theologies; they cannot escape thinking the *unum,* indeed, they draw their life precisely from passion for the *unum,* even though they conceal and display it in different ways. The true soul of the pluralist theories is not so much the assertion of pluralism, which in the case of the religions is an incontrovertible fact, as it is the search for a reconciliation, that is, for some unifying point that would permit the correlation and coexistence of all religions. The authentic "pluralist" is in reality a lover of unity. It may be a plural unity, but it is a unity nonetheless. Plurality is an obvious fact; the point is to interpret

---

8. The new theologies of religious pluralism have necessitated a new reflection on the topic of truth: W. Kasper, "Das Wahrheitsverständnis der Theologie," in *Theologie und Kirche,* vol. 2 (Mainz, 1999), 28-50; M. Seckler, "Theologie der Religionen mit Fragezeichen," *Theologische Quartalschrift* 166 (1986): 164-84; A. Kreiner, "Die Relevanz der Wharheitsfrage für die Theologie der Religionen," *Münchener theologische Zeitschrift* 41 (1990): 21-42; Kreiner, *Ende der Wharheit? Zum Wahrheitsverständnis in Philosophie und Theologie* (Freiburg, 1991); E. Arens, "Zur Struktur theologischer Wharheit," *Zeitschrift für katholische Theologie* 112 (1990): 1-17; A. Milano, *Quale verità. Per una critica della ragion teologica* (Bologna, 1999); E. Coreth, ed., *Wahrheit in Einheit und Vielheit* (Düsseldorf, 1987). Indications can also be found in M. Henry, *C'est moi la verité* (Paris, 1996).

it in a way that unites rather than disjoins. Stated in the most general terms, the pluralists' enterprise is to develop an adequate hermeneutics of plurality in order to ground the de facto plurality of religions in a de jure plurality and, therefore, more or less consciously, in a unitary "first principle"[9] that in their view underlies de facto plurality. On the supposition that pluralism is an unproblematic interiorization of a plurality that already exists in fact, pluralist theology is obliged to provide arguments for this interiorization in order to attain its goal of a plurality free from absurd absolutist claims and, as such, no longer apt to generate conflict.

If a good pluralist is bound to work out a clear model of unity, the next question that arises is: What kind of unity shall it be? This question also has to do with what accounts for unity and where it is achieved. As for the first point, the question is whether the plurality of religions can be reconciled without prejudice to particular affiliations and identities; is there some higher perspective that recapitulates all the religions while respecting their differences? Is the correlation of the religions religious? Can we then reasonably envisage a religious meeting of religions, an encounter of religions on a specifically religious level, without the need for a lowest, or highest, common denominator? Or must we conceive this encounter in terms of the development of interrelations among human beings and, therefore, in function of some sociopolitical model? A final possibility would be to try various combinations of these three proposals, without of course claiming to be exhaustive. In any case, the pluralist should be able to answer the question about what the religions are supposed to agree about: Is the point of convergence ethical, intellectual, political, religious, or global?

The second question is whether the encounter that supposedly confirms or manifests the hitherto hidden compatibility of religions occurs within a cultural and political framework that permits and, in some respects, demands such an encounter, or whether the individual's consciousness and interiority are the "locus" of the exchange and harmonization of experiences of plurality.

Naturally, both answers can exist within each other. Not only do they not cancel each other out, they even reinforce each other. John Hick's system differs from Knitter's on this point. Hick tends to situate the *unum* in

---

9. The question concerns the nature of this principle: Is it intellectual, religious, political, moral, or all these things at once?

an Ultimate Reality, which is decentered with respect to the human spirit and, therefore, in an external and impersonal medium. Knitter, by contrast, places it within the human spirit — an identification, he insists, that can be experienced in every religion without exception. The individual subject represents both unity and plurality in himself.[10] In Knitter the subject is "capable" of pluralism and, as such, functions as the unifying principle in which diversity is preserved and overcome.

Precisely because he must willy-nilly conceive plurality in terms of a one, while being willing to allow every sort of contradiction, the pluralist must sooner or later come clean about how he understands truth. As soon as they conceive the idea of the *unum*, pluralist theologians find themselves offering some sort of account of how we approach the *verum*. Metaphysics, thrown out by the front door, sneaks back in through the window. Let us try to explain, then, why truth matters for a correct understanding of plurality.

The transcendental *verum* brings into play all the threads of relation within which man actually lives: his relationship with God,[11] with other human beings, with himself, and with the world. From the phenomenological point of view, the event of interpersonal relation obviously stands at the experiential origin of man's perception and reasoning.[12] It is from within this

10. P. F. Knitter, *Una terra molte religioni. Dialogo religioso e responsabilità globale* (Assisi, 1998), 233-62; Knitter, *Nessun altro nome? Un esame critico degli atteggiamenti cristiani verso le religioni mondiali* (Brescia, 1991), 196ff. According to John Hick, the distinctive feature of religious experience is a passage from self-centeredness to other-centeredness. This religious experience is necessary for the relationship with the Ultimate Reality, but it cannot be identified with the irreducible and unknowable transcendence of the "Real in itself." See J. Hick, *An Interpretation of Religion: Human Responses to the Transcendent* (New Haven, 1989), 236.

11. The great medieval doctors approached the *quaestio de veritate* in terms of a relation to an eternal truth and saw the human intellect as related to the divine intellect. For Thomas Aquinas, in particular, truth has a fivefold root: (1) the relation of things to the Creator *(creatio)*; (2) the human intellect's relation to itself *(reflexio)*; (3) the human intellect's relation to things *(adaequatio)*; (4) the human intellect's relation the divine intellect *(actus, apprehensio, lumen)*; (5) the relation of identity and subsistence characterizing the divine intellect in itself. Thanks to this fivefold root, there is a relation of truth with all things, truth is knowable, truth can be recognized by all, truth is linked with the truth of oneself (perfectionism), and there is an eternal, immutable truth.

12. H. U. von Balthasar offers what, in my opinion, is still the best available treatment of the interpersonal dimension of truth in H. U. von Balthasar, *Theo-Logic. Theological Logical Theory. I: Truth of the World* (San Francisco, 2001). For an overview of the transcendentals, see H. U. von Balthasar, *Epilog* (Einsiedeln, 1987).

relationship that man finds access to his own interiority, to the outside world, and in a conscious way to the transcendence of God, even though this latter relation is the most basic. In order to follow the unfolding of the logic of the *verum* as the truth of man, the truth of the world, and the truth of God, we must retrace, at least in broad outlines, the genealogy of truth within the genealogy of man.

a. The origin is an event of interpersonal communion that remains fundamental for how we understand the nature of truth, and that is primarily metaphysical and not just psychological. In this original event man is placed before something absolute and incontrovertible: the good that is another's love. Man simply draws life and nourishment from this good, which for him is as immediate as being. Nothing — no thought or decision — stands between him and his good. On the contrary, every subsequent thought and decision is possible precisely because of this primordial, unconditioned reality, which neither thought nor decision can ever fully retrieve, for it is a gratuitousness that, without even asking our consent, squanders itself on us. The solidity and absoluteness of this beginning provide man in his infancy with the experiential, if not the ontological, principle of his "I," and therefore the principle of thought. They represent, in a certain sense, the "primary truth" of man's own being, the point beyond which he cannot regress without entering a different order of reality, whether higher (God) or lower (worldly nature).[13] We take for granted that there can be no truth until we find principles that no longer stand in need of further principles for their justification. Such principles, moreover, must function as the criterion of the *verum*. The man who can recognize through reflection the sequence that we have outlined can be said to possess a criterion of truth that enables him to judge what is presented to him in the world of interpersonal relationships. The organization of abstract thought, hence the capacity to recognize and to make one's own a grammar and a syntax, logical norms and principles, rises only upon this foundation and never stands without it. Evidently the link between the two levels is not simply accidental. The first principles are based on absolutely undeniable (and in fact, never denied) evidences that constitute the "I" and thought, whose seat is communication from person to person.

13. For a fuller treatment of this theme, see my *Natura della comunione. Saggio sulla relazione* (Soveria Mannelli, 1999).

b. Access to the *verum* is given, secondarily, through the intellect and reason — secondarily because, as we have already said, the faculties of understanding and reason are not the *primum,* inasmuch as they are activated upon the abiding foundation of a dynamic that embraces them on all sides, and not merely *a parte ante.* From a metaphysical point of view, then, intellect cannot be the beginning and end of truth, because intellect always already finds itself in a broader context. We cannot speak meaningfully of "truth" unless we can see, or at least glimpse, the major premise of the entire process.

If we look closely at the genesis of spirit at the dawn of man's life, we realize that he does not owe this spirit to his parents (or their surrogates). It is simply a contradiction to imagine that an "I" could produce another, unique "I." It can be easily demonstrated philosophically that man is not the product of man, nor is it unreasonable to admit an "Other" who confers on man, on each man, his identity, along with the rationality inherent in it.

At the beginning of the chain of truth there should be a primary truth. But truth begins to take shape from within personal relationship. If, then, human persons do not originate human persons, they cannot originate the chain of truth. There must, then, be a communion of Persons that seals, and fully embodies, the truth that dawns within the interpersonal relation we have described. This reasoning follows from the intrinsic link between person and truth. This suggests that the intellect's movement of transcendence is nothing but an echo, albeit a significant one, of the transcendence of the divine persons over human persons in the dynamic of their relational being. If the affirmation of God falls, the affirmation of man's identity and of the coherence of truth falls with it.

c. Another *conditio sine qua non* of truth is the intellect's relationship with itself. This relationship, too, is originally rooted in the relationship with others and with God, which is a form of spiritual interiority. Many authors over the course of the centuries have pointed out the intrinsically dialogical nature of the human spirit, which among Christian thinkers is seen in terms of the enstatic relationship of persons. Nicholas of Cusa explains man's self-knowledge as a participation in God's vision and knowledge of man.[14] Even before him, Thomas Aquinas had presented the *reditio* as the specific feature of spiritual creatures and, significantly, had

14. Nicholas of Cusa, *De visione Dei.*

linked it with ontological proximity to God: the closer a creature is to God, the more it is capable of a full *reditio.*[15]

This third condition suggests that man's entire subjectivity is engaged in the question of truth, not so much because of the involvement of freedom but because of the ontology of subjectivity itself.

d. The last aspect of relationality concerns man's (and his intellect's) relation to reality and to the world. This relation also pertains to truth. Man always reaches truth that resides in the objects and the situations he encounters in everyday life. His knowledge proceeds by degrees of adequation. But this progression must not be interpreted, as in some epistemologies of science, in a solely negative way; it is not so much an inbuilt deficiency as an unveiling that opens analogously to the greatest mystery: that of the Creator. At the same time, this type of truth should not be inflated into a paradigm, as has unfortunately commonly happened in many currents of European thought for the last several centuries. To do so is to subvert the order that obtains among the different types of knowledge. We must, in short, avoid confusing consent on this level of knowing with true universality. We are, after all, dealing with a lower domain of reality; even presupposing its general accessibility to the common understanding, this domain cannot be the seat of such universality.[16]

That having been said, we must beware of divorcing the truth from the world by hiding or denying the sign-character of worldly reality. The world, including the world of physical things, with its manifold forms and functions, rhythms and dynamisms, its microscopic and macroscopic constitution, is a "book" whose perusal can always teach us something new. Of course, we cannot learn if we begin and end in the world alone. But this is impossible if one enters the logic of the truth. As Albert Einstein once remarked to a student: "God is subtle, but he is not a liar." His point, of course, is that there is an inner reliability in the syntax that governs the universe. All human beings can discern this syntax and follow its main

15. Thomas Aquinas, *De spiritualibus creaturis.* See C. Fabro, *Percezione e pensiero* (Milan, 1941); J. A. Izquierdo Labeaga, *La vita intellettiva* (Vatican City, 1994); M. d'Avenia, *La conoscenza per connaturalità* (Bologna, 1992); G. Busiello, "Conoscenza abituale di sé e conoscenza immediata dell'esistenza di Dio in san Tommaso," *Sapienza* 52 (1999): 317-56.

16. A certain epistemological monism has filled the void left by the collapsing distinction between God, man, and the world or cosmos. Only this collapse could make sense of statements such as "we come to know God by the light of nature, just as we come to know geometry" (H. More, *An Antidote Against Atheisme* 1 [London, 1653], 10, 31).

lines. They thereby touch an objective validity that carries a certain spiritual value as well.

Our brief sketch of the preconditions of the *verum* suggests that truth is located on three different levels: the cosmic, the human, and the divine. This distinction of registers calls for explanation. Which raises the following question: What role does the *verum* (and its interpersonal matrix) play in the pluralism of cultures and religions? This question bears the weight of a double failure: the failure of late medieval culture to meet the challenge of humanism and the failure of Enlightenment rationalism to resist inversion into terrorism (French Revolution) and totalitarianism (Nazism, communism).[17] Does a return to the question of truth require a retrieval of the Enlightenment's concept of universality? Would not an ethical foundation be more promising? But isn't this precisely what the Deists and the English freethinkers attempted already in the 1600s?[18]

Plurality in the Truth or Plurality of Truths?

The conditions under which creatures attain unity in the truth are uniform, but their explicit unfolding in the order of knowledge involves a variety of clearly distinct forms. To confuse these forms, to subsume them under some supposedly comprehensive category, is inimical to a precise understanding of the *verum*. In particular, such a move makes it difficult to grasp the anthropological and interpersonal significance of truth as a medium of relationality. What man can easily know can be taken as a basis for a mutual recognition. But how do we know, how do we recognize one another according to truth?

Let us begin our answer by examining the lowest form of access to the truth, that is, the logical-mathematical, which is characteristic of the natural sciences. Both mathematics and natural science yield a series of statements falling within the scope of certain procedures that any student of

17. Cf. M. Horkheimer and T. W. Adorno, *Dialettica dell'illuminismo* (Turin, 1974).

18. The pluralists' underlying tendency to identify morality and religion can be seen in such authors as W. Wollaston, C. Blount, T. Morgan, M. Tindal (among others). Wollaston writes: "If there is a moral good and evil . . . there is religion; and this religion can be called 'natural.' By 'religion' I mean nothing but an obligation to do . . . what should not be left undone and to abstain from what should not be done" (*The Religion of Nature Delineated* [London, 1724], 25). See Byrne, 61-69.

them endowed with sufficient talent and knowledge can easily understand. But neither mathematics nor natural science is an adequate medium of interpersonal relations, inasmuch as logic and mathematics are based on the "laws of the mind" while the natural sciences pertain to the cosmos. Neither the truth of reason and intellect nor of intracosmic reality can comprehend the totality of the human person. By the same token, neither can legitimately function as a medium of relation; neither can bring together a plurality that goes beyond the mind and the cosmos.[19] To be sure, even this level of knowing offers a degree of objectivity that can serve as a foundation for a certain consensus. But this consensus gets its shape from the specificity of the *verum* on which it depends. For the same reason, no community or society has ever been erected on the basis of the mathematical and/or scientific *verum*, which cannot sustain and justify societies such as the family, the polis, or the relationship among cultures and peoples.

We have next to consider a kind of truth that by nature involves the whole of the human being and thus brings his freedom into play. This order of truth is clearly distinct from the one we have just considered. The knowledge that is proper to it can also be formally distinguished from mathematical or scientific cognition. If someone were to assert that man is a being who transcends the world and were to demonstrate this claim rationally, he himself would thereby be evidencing a truth about himself, and whoever might affirm or deny his claim would perforce evidence a truth about himself. Truth claims about the reality of man cannot be accepted without creating a certain communion between those who advance them and those who intelligently and freely admit their truth. This modality of truth does not merely mediate their relationship like an air that everyone breathes but that remains substantially different from him. This type of truth is not merely impersonal. All participate in the truth, but always as something that is inherent in each, in one's "I," one's humanity in its integrity, and therefore in all human beings. Here we can think of truth as a factor of interpersonality and therefore of bringing the many into unity, just as knowledge of a truth about man leads to the recognition of man in himself and in others.

The potential for communion is linked to the faculty for truth that all men share and to the truth that it attains. The fact of sharing a faculty and

19. Here "intellect" also means a part of the spiritual reality of man that can go by the same name.

of recognizing it as such exhibits the dialogical nature, and therefore relational quality, of the faculty itself. The truth can never finally be separated from truthfulness, and thus from trustworthiness, and so from trust and faith.[20] The truth is "personal."[21] The attainment of truth especially brings the ontological aspect of communion to light: truth is the truth of being. Given the inseparability of these two aspects, we can conclude that truth is the truth of personal being.[22]

This raises anew the question as to whether this "truth," this kind of *verum,* both unites and differentiates, whether it is what enables us to speak meaningfully of plurality and unity. Are we substituting a humanistic Enlightenment for an intellectualist one? The universality of the *communio personarum* for the universality of intellect and reason? What is the purpose of this hidden *reductio ad anthropologiam* in relation to the pluralistic theology of religions?

Regarding the first question, all human beings are given a capacity to access truth and an identical nature, albeit one variously configured by differences of language, people, and culture. The diversity of interpretations[23]

20. H. U. von Balthasar writes: "This reduction of knowledge of the truth to a purely theoretical evidence drained of all vital personal and ethical decisions so palpably narrows the scope of truth that it *ipso facto* loses its universality and, therefore, its very essence" (Balthasar, *Theo-Logic,* 28). On the other hand, once it is recognized that truth occurs only within the personal exchange and communion, the question of truthfulness becomes fundamental. "The word that he [the speaker] has pronounced is no longer a mere expression of the internal word but a *testimony.* The speaker establishes an equation between the content and the form of his utterance. The equation cannot be checked over from the outside; the speaker vouches for the correctness of the equation. In vouching for this as a person, he creates for the receiver a substitute for its missing ability to verify. The declaration of truth thus becomes a kind of deposition, and as such it implies the ethical characteristic of truthfulness. By the same token, there is a corresponding *faith* on the part of the receiver. Without this faith, any exchange of truth between free entities is unthinkable" (96). See also B. Stubenrauch, *Dialogisches Dogma. Der christliche Auftrag zur interreligiösen Begegnung* (Freiburg, 1995), 34-68.

21. John Hick writes: "The Real an sich cannot be said to be personal" (Hick, *An Interpretation of Religion,* 264).

22. Ignace de la Potterie's masterpiece, *La verité dans Saint Jean* (Rome, 1977), shows how the biblical tradition, unlike that of classical Greece, has an interpersonal understanding of truth. Andrea Milano corroborates de la Potterie's philological demonstration in a christocentric key in *Quale verità* (see n. 8).

23. Hick's argument that religious differences are ultimately differences on the level of hermeneutics or of conceptualization is reminiscent of the theory of the linguistic origin of religions proposed by John Toland and developed by Max Müller.

of the same data is ultimately less important than the ability to know the data themselves, or even more, a greater truth that, if not present, is at least obscurely glimpsed in actual experience. Human nature is not something static and fixed. While its essence remains incontrovertible, it lends itself to a dynamization, either in the direction of truth or in the direction of its vital denial. Because of this the plurality of hermeneutic viewpoints,[24] of interpretations of the same data, is less fundamental than the diversification of the data themselves (which does not, of course, take away the basic unity that exists among human beings). Think, for instance, of the process of personal identification, of "personalization," because of which, after original sin, man stands in need of another who can reveal to him the truth about himself. To the extent that this personalizing factor has not yet entered into the life of a man, of a people, or of a culture, there is a corresponding weakening not of the sense of personhood but of its objective reality. The same can be said of everything that is properly human in man.

From this point of view, Hick's reduction of plurality to the hermeneutic principle seems to be vitiated by an initial simplification — the inevitable consequence of forgetfulness of the *verum* and of human beings' innate capacity for truth. A hermeneutic of subjective idealism supplants the realism of the *verum*.[25] Both communion and difference are diminished by the introduction of hermeneutics as the explanatory criterion of plurality. Any commonality, in Hick's model, is as fixed as it is inaccessible. It is something that exists "in itself" and to which we refer without ever truly attaining it. What is common can be common only on the condition that no one really participates in it. This becomes apparent when one considers Hick's problematic notion of revelation.[26] But even plurality loses its reality and consistency. Since everyone gathers something of the Real "in itself," everyone's identity consists precisely in his diversity from the others. It remains very clear that none can attain the reality. Thus, just as the

24. The hermeneutical model plays an enormous role in the pluralistic theologies of religion, so much so, in fact, that these theologies could be understood as the outcome of a rigorous application of nineteenth- and twentieth-century hermeneutics to religion, both as a phenomenon to interpret and as the product of interpretation.

25. Paul Knitter agrees with his critic, George Lindbeck, on this point: "the experiences which religions evoke and mold are as varied as the interpretative schema." Cited in Knitter, *Una terra molte religioni*, 83.

26. G. Gäde, *Viele Religionen — ein Wort Gottes. Einspruch gegen John Hicks pluralistische Religionstheologie* (Gütersloh, 1998), particularly 124-34.

colors of the spectrum can form a rainbow only if there is no interchange among them, the plurality of positions depends on their fixity, not on the acknowledgment of a "more" that entails not only a change of consciousness (I am aware of being a band of the spectrum and therefore a part of the whole), but also a conversion of being. In reality the logic of truth under the impulse of real being in its actuality tends toward an excess that is not dreamed up in some hermeneutical fancy, but is required by the mystery that has made itself present, and therefore by its own objectivity. The logic of the *verum* thus carries a different conception both of plurality and of unity. By the same token, the *verum* imposes itself on the *unum*, thus becoming its very center.

According to this vision that comes forth from the observance of the *verum*, unity and plurality acquire meaning only in truth. Outside truth, even plurality remains groundless and cannot have any grounds at all, whether we mean the plurality of persons, of cultures, or of religions. If we remain outside of this veritable consideration in which occurs the connection with truth, and if at the same time the Enlightenment's account of plurality and unity is discarded, spiritualism can appear to fill the resulting vacuum in the absence of a return to the question of truth. In that case an intellectualist Enlightenment that repudiates religion as a usurper of the rights of reason gives way to an Enlightenment that critiques religion in the name of the religions, that abandons reason's claim to truth, that appeals to a gnostic spiritualism tinged with a voluntarism and humanitarianism tied to the logic of a certain political velleity. The critique of religion that seemed to have been completed by the young Hegelians reappears in a new form with the theologians of religious pluralism, who, understanding religion as a form of consciousness (hermeneutics), are the legitimate heirs of the worst fruits of a marriage between classic German idealism and early English Deism.

We do not intend to propose a humanistic enlightenment in place of the intellectualistic version of the eighteenth century or the spiritualistic variation of the second half of the twentieth. We are aware of diversity and realize that access to the *verum* could be blocked and rendered difficult by any number of circumstances.[27] We confirm the creatural chance as an inescapable

27. A recent issue of the journal *Paradosso* (2/3, 1997) on the subject of truth contains over thirty contributions by theologians and philosophers belonging to various schools. It thus offers a colorful portrait of the multiplicity of current approaches to truth.

basis of every encounter in our creaturely condition. Every attempt to bypass the question of truth or to limit its scope necessarily opens the way to various types of fraud, whether they be ideologically utopian, spiritually gnostic, intellectualistically antihumanist, or voluntaristically humanitarian.

By now, history has made it clear that it is no easier to agree about man than about God. The peoples and cultures of the West, after having abandoned God and experienced the consequent destruction of man, now seek refuge with spiritual entities that not only have nothing to do with the "old God" (Dostoyevsky's Kirilov), but are actually opposed to him.[28] Indeed, even consensus about man, which had rested on the foundations of Christian faith and experience, is dangerously tottering. Thus, if rejection of the answer obscures the clarity of the question, the search for a false answer often goes along with the posing of a false or distorted question. That question is man.

The last objection concerns the emphasis on man's creatureliness that follows from an interpretation of the transcendentals within an account of being as communion.

This shift aims methodologically, on the one hand, at retrieving a clear distinction between man's being and the being of the world and, on the other hand, at underscoring the extent to which the truth of the encounter between men, cultures, and religions must pass through human nature in all its breadth, without falling into the illusion of being able to comprehend it from the height of a superior principle (gnosticism) or a collective spirit (Averroism). Man cannot encounter man in truth merely on the level of humanity, since "man infinitely surpasses man" (Pascal), but neither can he truly encounter his fellow man apart from his human nature. In the first approach the religious sense would have no role to play in interpersonal encounter; in the second the religious encounter could take concrete form only on the level of religion. Both paradigms are guilty of partiality.

---

28. It is a paradox that the very culture that has criticized Catholicism as "pagano-papist" and has branded every form of Christianity that goes beyond "natural" religion as "sectarian" has given birth to huge sects that today spread their tentacles throughout the world. This proliferation of cults seems to raise some questions for the pluralistic theology of religions. The most acute critics of this theology have put their finger on its lack of criteria for discernment among true and false religions; many local governments can testify that this same lack sometimes threatens to tear apart the fabric of society itself. A characteristic shared by all cults is a denigration of man's natural dignity as a creature of God.

To a certain extent the remedy we have tried to offer requires recognition that the dynamic of the truth and of adequation to truth involves a going beyond toward the Other and others.[29] Our proposal is not to replace religion as a locus of a merely possible encounter with the truth as the locus of an already actual, albeit not fully or concretely recognized one. Our point is rather that we cannot realistically sustain the hypothesis of plurality — even of a plurality of religions — outside of the truth. Religions are not in fact entities in their own right. What really exists are religious men, and the encounter among religions is merely an encounter among human beings who adhere to this or that religion. We have therefore tried to bring the noun (man) back into play, while avoiding a surreptitious and dangerous substitution of the noun with the adjective (religious). It is to this latter that we now turn.

Homo Religiosus

Man is indisputably a religious being. How does membership in a religion define the relationship among men, cultures, and peoples? Is the relationship somehow religious? Is a pluralistic theology of religions admissible? Where does it get the panoramic and, indeed, lofty vantage point it brings to the question? Isn't the pluralistic theology of religions the fruit of the greatest presumption, inasmuch as it places itself beyond the claims *of* truth in order to harmonize different claims *to* truth?[30]

29. Emmanuel Lévinas remains a paradigm on this point. From beginning to end, Lévinas shows no trace either of a naturalistic humanism or a rationalistic, idealistic, spiritualist religiosity.

30. A number of pluralist authors argue from the point of view of God, or of a divine plan, in order to explain the actual plurality of religions. In this respect the pluralists are faithful heirs of their Deist forebears. Historically speaking, this argument presupposes a move from the affirmation of the *religio naturalis* to the claim that it is identical with *theologia naturalis,* which is to say, *theologia rationalis.* This identification could never have occurred without an understanding of religion as a form of thought and of revelation as something reducible to the operations of an autonomous, disinhabited mind. By the same token, this identification — and therefore, its offspring known as the pluralistic theology of religions — is impossible so long as man is considered as a whole, and not primarily as a pure intellectuality; they are out of the question so long as his interiority, spirit, and mind are understood as always already existing in communion with, and as inhabited by, the Creator. If, in fact, it is man, and not primarily or solely his reason, who is caught up in the dy-

Let us begin by looking at the category of "religion." It is commonly used to indicate a variety of disparate realities. The umbrella of "religion" covers radically diverse things. Religion is what arises from the recognition of a divine subjectivity (as in Judaism, Christianity, and Islam), or perhaps of several subjectivities (Hinduism). Or else it is what, in the absence of a relationship with a superior and transcendent subject, wisely guides the practitioner toward a metaphysical, transcendental reality (Buddhism, Taoism). But religion is also the province of those who practice a mediumistic or magical relation with otherworldly entities or spirits, as in animism, channeling, and the like. It may even designate organizations that have to do with "religious issues" but whose primary modus operandi takes place on the level of finance, marketing, and information (Scientology, Jehovah's Witnesses, Moonies, and so forth). The impressive fresco of religions spread across the inhabited earth seems unequivocally to suggest the presence of a religious dimension in man, and more problematically and uncertainly, the existence of a presence or presences that reveal it or themselves to man and with which he perhaps communicates. We will consider the first aspect: man's religious sense.

The religious sense seems to be man's fundamental instinct. It exists in addition to, and alongside of, the pleasure principle, the instinct for self-preservation, and the death wish that share residence in man's inner being. We leave open the question of its locus: Is it situated on the same level as the intrapsychic factors just mentioned, or does it exist on a higher level that we could call "spiritual"? What is pretty generally admitted is that it cuts across the whole reality of the human person and informs man in his entirety. Hence its strategic value when one talks, in global terms, of "unifying the human family." Whereas the global was once conceived in terms of a common reason and, still more recently, in terms of a "planetary ethics" (H. Küng), there is a growing awareness today of the political need for a religious globalism, which is not, of course, the same as a global religion

namism of religion, his *desiderium Dei naturale (religio naturalis)* remains essentially distinct from his own reflection on religion *(theologia naturalis)*. And if his interiority is inhabited *(oikesis)*, then the revelation of the one who inhabits it cannot be reduced to such reflection. On the contrary, this revelation can modify the intrinsic potentiality of human interiority, not only without denaturing man, but in such a way as to bring him into the fullness of his truth (incarnation, resurrection, ascension). It follows, then, that it is simply absurd, even as a postulate, to absorb *theologia revelata* into *theologia naturalis* or *religio revelata* in *religio naturalis.*

or a totalitarianism of religion itself. This suggests the urgent need to re-think the nature and role of the religious sense and of the different ways of understanding and responding to it.[31] This formulation of the question already distances us from the theologians of religious pluralism, who understand the multiplicity of religions not as a variety of answers to one and the same question, but as so many culturally and historically differentiated ways of revealing and interpreting the one divinity or Ultimate Reality. In the pluralist account, all forms of interpreting the question add all the answers that man invents or discovers are from on high. In this way the clear line of demarcation between the creaturely question and the divine answer disappears. The mere act of taking the question seriously supposedly itself guarantees the answer.[32]

This suggests the fruitlessness of shifting dialogue with the theologies of religious pluralism onto the level of the answers, that is, the specifically theological and christological level, without a prior clarification of the prior level of creatureliness. The fact that Judeo-Christian revelation begins with creation should also have a methodological significance, even if, from a historical point of view, we can speak of man and of man's religious sense as we do only in virtue of the revelation of man contained in the Old Testament and in Jesus Christ. We do not infer from this, of course, the fu-

31. David Pailin distinguishes nine meanings of the term *religio naturalis* in use between the sixteenth and twentieth centuries. It has meant: (1) an intellectually grounded religious conviction that is accessible to every man and whose truth can be verified rationally; (2) the religion that Adam received from God and that, in one way or another, was then passed on to the whole human race (once this religion, consisting of truths disclosed by God, has been identified, it can function as a criterion for measuring all other religions); (3) an invention of man, the origin, center, and goal of religion; (4) religious beliefs and practices accessible to empirical study; (5) the religion of man in the "state of nature," uninfluenced by civilization ("the noble savage"); (6) what is common in the world's different empirical religions (Kant's "substrate of all religions"); (7) a human faculty for the infinite analogous to man's faculty for the finite; (8) the values and behaviors of those who live by principles and models taken from nature; (9) the religion whose center is the power of the natural world (D. Pailin, "Theologie und Religionsphilosophie vom 17. Jahrhundert bis zur Gegenwart," in *Theologische Realenzyklopädie* 24, pp. 78ff.). Curiously, Pailin does not mention the Catholic definition of natural religion. On this topic see H. de Lubac, *Il mistero del sovrannaturale* (Milan, 1978); de Lubac, *Spirito e libertà* (Milan, 1980); de Lubac, *La rivelazione divina e il mistero dell'uomo* (Milan, 1985); H. U. von Balthasar, "Il movimento verso Dio," in *Spiritus Creator* (Brescia, 1972), 11-48.

32. For de Lubac's account of this point, see M. Figura, *Der Anruf der Gnade. Über die Beziehung des Menschen zu Gott nach Henri de Lubac* (Einsiedeln, 1979).

tility of carrying the discussion to the specifically christological plane. Our point is simply that we cannot do so without an anthropological and metaphysical comparison as well.

Pluralist theologians appeal to what they call "religious experience" rather than to the religious sense. Apparently this experience is supposed to represent the point of contact between the human and the transcendent. It is here that the pluralists seek the traces of a possible encounter with, and acknowledgment of, religions. The point is not so much an actual exchange as it is the creation of space in which one can, so to say, put himself in the other's shoes and vice versa (Knitter).

The shift from the religious sense to so-called religious experience allows pluralist theologians to assert, at one and the same time, the approximation to the divine and the mutual irreducibility of religious experiences, two factors that supposedly eliminate conflict among truth claims. According to the Indian parable cited by Hick,[33] we are all like blind men touching a different part of the elephant; everyone forms a general idea from his own experience, but no one really knows what an elephant is, even though everyone is talking about the same beast. We arrive at a very different outcome if we assume the religious sense as a question present in all human beings and proceed according to the logic of the *verum* that was described above. In this approach we do not presuppose contact with the divine. By the same token, it gives the plausible and practicable means for conducting an objective discussion that an ineffable "experience" does not.[34]

According to the pluralists, the source of the conflict that undermines universal harmony is not so much religious experience as its interpretation, which is elaborated with a claim to truth that, as such, arrogates to itself the right to exclude or include other "truths." The conflict of religions is, in their view, a conflict of interpretations; religious experience itself is strongly marked by the hermeneutics of the subject, albeit with reference to an objectivity common to all (the elephant of the parable). The pluralist account thus posits two common elements: the hermeneutic structure of the human spirit and the Ultimate Reality to which this structure refers.

---

33. Hick, *God and the Universe of Faiths: Essays in the Philosophy of Religion* (London, 1973), 140.

34. J. Dupuis, *Verso una teologia cristiana del pluralismo religioso* (Brescia, 1997), 326: "Religious experience is, by its nature, ineffable."

The Ultimate Reality cannot be affected in any way. What can be affected, however, is the activity of understanding the Ultimate Reality, which bestows on it the form that then gives shape to the various religions. What was a cause of disunity can, with the introduction of a further and more nuanced interpretation, become a cause of pluralistic reconciliation. In this way there can a priori be no mistake, or correction, in the "religious experience." Error can occur only at the level of secondary reflection, on the level of theological argumentation, inasmuch as one tries to apply a conceptual scheme to religious experience as a whole and, on that basis, to compare it to other experiences. It is therefore impossible to distinguish a religion from a cult or pseudoreligious organization, with all the consequences that follow for society and politics.

The pluralist theology of religions claims, then, to introduce a hermeneutical corrective that, without removing differences, eliminates the pretensions to absoluteness that are at the root of divisions and conflicts. By the same token it presents itself as part of a global theory of interrelation,[35] the acceptance of which supposedly enables the birth of a new universal peace. If differences among religious experiences are rooted in different activities of the human spirit, the establishment of peace through the acknowledgment of pluralism will also result from a change of consciousness, a more complete understanding, a more complex hermeneutical act. The harmony among religions cannot be found in the religions themselves, which are different and mutually irreducible as such, but in a "theology of religions," that is, from the superior perspective of a higher plane of abstraction. The application of a practical, ethical, or liberationist varnish does nothing to change the underlying logic of this position. Indeed, the application is made necessary by the basic premise: the pluralists presuppose a dualistic conception of religion. Religion is an activity (or passivity) of the spirit to which a social praxis must then be added.

The question of the role of religion and of religious affiliation in the encounter of men, peoples, and cultures remains open. In the models proposed by the pluralists, religious identity plays an essential part in the establishment of a planetary alliance. This centering on religious identity has

35. It is on this level that we face the challenge of finding conceptions and experiences capable of embracing the whole human family. Modern thought is characterized by repeated efforts to construct a global theory of interrelation. Hitherto, these efforts have mostly been social or political, but not explicitly religious. Of course, Russian universalistic theories of *sobornost'* are an exception to this rule.

been criticized as unreal and utopian.[36] The pluralists do not preach the necessity of disavowing one's religious identity. Instead, they base interreligious dialogue on the admission of the equal dignity of each religion — not, however, on the recognition of a creaturely nature or on the critical comparison of the different answers that, following different trajectories and methods, human beings have given to the question of God. The different religions are different itineraries toward the same common salvation, and they must be recognized as religions (Knitter's "passing over"). The mutual recognition of religions is in this case "religious." Insofar as it is religious, every religious path can recognize another religion simply because it is a religion. Doctrinal, ritual, or moral specificities are not the immediate object of this recognition, but are subsumed under the category of the "religious."

Neither the "logical" nor the "religious" model of pluralism is convincing as the centerpiece of a general theory of relation. It is by no means obvious how one could go about instituting "religious," to say nothing of "logical," relation among individuals or peoples. Inasmuch as man's identity is not primarily logical or religious (as the pluralists understand these terms), even though it is always also both, we need to see that the kinds of relations man has depend on the kind of identity. Man's identity is creaturely and is therefore the work of Another. His personal identity, explained only by the bond the Creator has established with him, takes shape in the communion of persons. Therefore, relation must be sought on the level of man's natural and personal identity.[37] An approach to man that seeks the truth of his nature and personhood necessarily recognizes something of the work of God who makes himself known in them. In this way

36. See Knitter's examination of this approach in the first part of *Una terra molte religioni*.

37. A proposal of a global theory of relation that cannot offer any principled affirmation of the person and of personal identity must be seen as a potential support for totalitarianism. The weakness of all "global" social theories that do not appeal explicitly to the heritage and living tradition of Judaism and Christianity appears precisely in their failure to maintain with equal force the dignity of the person and the coessentiality of community. This weakness is due to a systematic forgetfulness of the religious, hence, transcendent dimension of man and of his relation to God. A one-sided retrieval of man's religious nature or, what is worse, of an apersonal religion, offers no way beyond this impasse, inasmuch as it leaves no way for the political dimension to enter except by way of an ideological juxtaposition lacking any compelling philosophical or theological rationale. The dividing line that cuts through man's inner being (religiosity/creatureliness) echoes also in the conflict between the I and the We.

the religious dimension comes into play, but not apart from the truth of man. Every dualistic account of the humanistic and religious aspects of relation fails to understand both. This is precisely the fate of the pluralistic theologies. These theologies juxtapose God and man, the truth of God (an "in itself" that is either beyond reach or else present in all religions in different ways) and the truth of man (the subject of a religious experience with no evident connection with his membership in the world). But, given this juxtaposition, there can be no truth.

The lethal division of the mystery of God from the mystery of man can be found expressed in two ways: either in man or in God himself. It occurs in man when he fails to admit and to acknowledge that, on a level deeper than any "religious experience," he is created in the image and likeness of God, possesses the divine breath in himself *(ruah)*, and is kept in existence by him, so that, without needing any "supernatural existential," man lives, moves, and has his being within an ontological belonging to his Lord and Creator. On this ontological level there is neither the immediate contact of a "religious experience" confused with free revelation nor a creaturely medium that somehow reaches the face and the name of the Creator.

The encounter cannot occur without the free action of God; another event has to take place. And yet man, in his reality, is inconceivable without God. A radical atheism is as unlikely as a literal theurgy. The mystery of creation is God's first covenant with man, and all created things bear, in every fiber of their being, this indelible seal. To misunderstand creation is to separate (unlawfully) man from God in man.

But there is another separation of the two that may be transferred in God. According to Christian theology, in the mystery of the eternal generation of the Son the Father expresses all, an all that includes the mystery of creation and, therein, of the creation of man. From this point of view man has always been in God. In Christ's resurrection and ascension into heaven in his true body, transfigured humanity is definitively seated at the right hand of the Father in its eschatological form. In God himself one finds the first and most important unity of God and man.

Misunderstanding the mystery of the most holy Trinity and of the incarnation means to sever man from God in God.

The line of demarcation that permanently distinguishes the creature as creature and the Creator as Creator cannot be effaced. Yet it has not prevented the manifestation and fulfillment of the close relationship between God and man and between man and God that the extraordinary event of the incarnation of the Logos has introduced at once into creation and into the divine life itself. And let no one separate not only what God has united, but what has been united in God. This marriage is indissoluble, without confusion or separation. It is immutable.

The marriage of God and man occurs in God and in man. On each side it has a specificity. Although they correspond to each other, these specificities are two distinct modes of relation and of the relational existence. Because of this, it is possible to deny one or the other, or else the specific unity of the two. The pluralists, who do not admit the distinction of the two modes, tend not so much to separate the two realities excessively or falsely as to unite them improperly. In the end the consistency of creaturely being dissolves in the ocean of the spiritual-religious, which is anything but a relationship between God and man in God.

The incarnation and the Trinity of hypostases, and the link between them, indicate precisely the path of identity and of relationality. The incarnation expresses the unity of the mystery of God with the mystery of man in the person of Jesus Christ. In him the truth of the first creation is revealed: only in him is man revealed to himself. But with the incarnation the manifestation of the extraordinary, and from now on, ordinary, unity of man and God reveals the other great mystery: God is a communion of persons. In doing so, it brings man into a relational potentiality that fulfills, while giving an entirely new meaning to, what man has received by nature. This event involves the whole of man's creaturely nature. It thus gives man a share in the life of God as communion. Both dimensions open at the same time to the greatest imaginable distinction, that between the divine hypostases, and to the greatest imaginable universality, that which embraces all men, all space, and all time.

When we consider the mysteries of Christianity, we realize that it not only fulfills but also surpasses the main aspirations of the pluralist theory. The fact of the matter is that in order to talk about plurality, one has to make use of some category under which to gather the homogeneous elements, in other words, one must make use of a notion of "unity." The kind of relationship pluralism envisages depends always and inevitably on the kind of unity to which it appeals. Because pluralist theologies weaken both creaturely and divine unity; because they almost entirely ignore their *connubium,* not only in redemption, but also in creation,[38] they end up di-

---

38. The soteriological reduction has a long history in Western theological thinking.

minishing, rather than enhancing, plurality itself. This outcome confirms the rule that the fuller the initial unity, the stronger the final plurality. Christians have the greatest advantage here, inasmuch as they begin with a unity that is already plural in itself.

Concluding Observations

In this brief reflection we have attempted to present a metaphysical and anthropological critique of the pluralistic theology of religions, with the aim of putting interreligious dialogue on a different and, in our opinion, even broader footing than do the pluralists themselves. Our guiding principle has been that man's religiosity is not simply the same as his nature, but that this nature cannot be understood correctly except in terms of its original creatureliness. Religiosity is innate in creatureliness, and by disregarding the latter, one loses any chance of truly understanding the former.

We based our attempted retrieval of creatureliness, whose scope we purposely limited, on the reevaluation of that mode of being called the *verum*. We expressed our disagreement with the limitations and restrictions of the pluralistic starting point, which, we saw, immediately links truth with a particular religion's claim to truth and tends to lade the very notion of truth with connotations of war, violence, or at the very least, conflict. On the first point we argued that the question of truth is broader than the question of the truth of a single religion, either in relation to others or in itself, and consequently that it is necessary to distinguish the *quaestio de veritate* from the question of the truth of a religion or of all religions. We are dealing with three different levels. One cannot meaningfully ask whether one religion is true with respect to others if one cannot ask whether it is true in itself. And we cannot ask about the truth of a religion in itself unless we can first ask about truth as such. A prior rejection of the *quaestio de veritate* renders meaningless the *quaestio de religionis veritate* or *de veritate religiosa*. This metaphysical, and thus philosophical, critique of the pluralistic theology of religions is in reality a metaphysical critique of a philosophy of religion disguising itself as a theology.[39]

---

39. We have already stopped to highlight the difficulties involved in the very concept of a "theology of religion" and in the (ultimately Hegelian) claim to see things from "God's point of view" (see n. 30).

We would like to conclude with some summary comments on (a) the dialectic between truth and peace; (b) the historical origins of the theology of pluralism; (c) the personalistic and communional character of truth; (d) the quality of universality and plurality.

a. A pseudoargument under cover of which the pluralists tend to eliminate surreptitiously the question of truth — and this brings us already to the second point — is that truth claims spawn war, legitimate the ideological supremacy of some over others, and discourage the possibility of a fruitful encounter with the diversity and otherness of different religions. To claim to stand for truth is ipso facto antithetical to tolerance and pluralism. Now this argument can work only if truth has ever done battle with itself. We find instead that truth fought against truth (albeit in the name of truth) only when the claim to truth armed itself with weapons other than those of the truth itself. The "critique of weapons," which is the mirror image of "the weapons of critique" in reverse, is not enough to attain the truth. In some cases it can be undertaken to fight off an aggressor, but then we are no longer dealing with the truth. The defeat of truth is not far off, indeed, has already occurred before the defender has entered the fray. Moreover, the two great totalitarian systems of the twentieth century, which wrought hitherto unprecedented destruction on humanity, both aggressively opposed the Judeo-Christian religion. Communist ideology proclaimed the overcoming of religion as early as the nineteenth century; once it became a system of power, it exerted every effort to achieve that aim. Nazism, attempting the physical elimination of the Jewish people, sought to wipe out the historical sign of God's covenant with man: the chosen people to whom revelation and the promise were given (J.-M. Lustiger).

Hannah Arendt's analysis of the logic of totalitarianism demonstrates that the dissolution of the European tradition, nihilism (the impossibility of a definitive, objectively knowable certainty), and atheism (the rejection of the supernatural) are the ingredients of totalitarian ideology.[40] The result has been the attempt to modify human nature, to demonstrate that man has no soul, that he is a superfluous being. Now since totalitarianism, from which the postmodernist is not entirely immune, originates in the denial of the truth, truth turns out to be antitotalitarian par excellence; and since the totalitarian denial of truth results in the manipulation of the human per-

40. For an account of Hannah Arendt's interpretation of the origin of totalitarianism, see M. Cangiotti, *L'ethos della politica. Studio su Hannah Arendt* (Urbino, 1990).

son, the assertion of the personal nature of man and of his original communionality is also a powerful antidote to all forms of totalitarianism, both present and future, clear and hidden. From this particular point of view we discover totalitarian elements in the theologies of religious pluralism, not only because they relativize truth, which they claim to divide up equally among the various religions, but above all because they deny its normative value for religious phenomenon, both on this side of it (metaphysics of creation), and on the other side (discernment of religions).

b. In reality, under the guise of promoting religious pluralism, the pluralist ideologies, taken in their main principles, gravely threaten the integrity of man's, especially Western man's, religious quest. They are, in fact, the true heirs of currents of thought whose classical expression is the English and French Enlightenment, but which go back even further to the Renaissance's *religio naturalis* and to English Deism. Just as the Enlightenment critique of religion is the end point of a development reaching back to the fifteenth and sixteenth centuries, the Enlightenment itself gave rise to another critique that aimed to carry out even more radically the aims of the Enlightenment. By the mid–nineteenth century certain thinkers began to declare the fulfillment of the deconstructive and destructive work that the Enlightenment had only glimpsed from afar. It was obvious that the radical crisis of religion would necessarily entail a corresponding anthropological shift; and given the advanced state of the crisis, the time had come to propose a valid alternative. This suggested a conceptual overcoming of religion by its dialectical inversion. Both Hegel and Marx, aware of the deficiencies in the Enlightenment's understanding of religion, sought, each in his own way, to remedy them, Hegel proclaiming the sublation of religion into other, more perfect forms, Marx prophesying the end of the religious era of humanity with the loss of the subjective and objective conditions that had produced it.

A century and a half later we can say that both Hegel and Marx have been proven wrong. At the beginning of the third millennium of the Christian era, the religious sense is flowering in a variety of disparate forms, and it gives no sign of metamorphosing into a higher form of consciousness, or of disappearing through a change in the material conditions of existence. People today seem resigned to live in peace, in one way or another, with the religious dimension of their being, even as they reserve the right to interpret it as they wish, if possible without the aid of prepackaged institutions and doctrines. This explains the success in the West of new "religious" concoctions and the willingness of many who have denied or forgotten their Christian roots to accept religious traditions imported from other countries and cultures.

In sum, we can say that the Enlightenment has, contrary to expectations, lost the gamble: the *homo religiosus* is alive and well, both in the East and in the West, in the North and in the South. Nevertheless, the present situation lends itself to interpretation in the sense of the first correctors of Enlightenment ideology (Hegel and the Hegelian left). The theologies of religious pluralism read it as requiring a change in our approach to religion. They argue for a shift to a different and (by implication) higher form of consciousness. This is the core of the pluralist proposal. Indeed, the method and content of the pluralist theologies are meant to be the heart of what is in effect a new ideology, the suprareligious, in other words "theological," form of a new religious consciousness.

This move makes the pluralist theologies the heirs of the Enlightenment critique of religion and of all the successive attempts to perfect it, attempts they propose to complete in our own day. The motto is: the dissolution of religion as an original fact of man's creaturely condition into the "religions." Not even Karl Marx hit on the idea that religions could act as solvents of religion, that the "theology" of religion could eliminate religion, that one spiritual entity could have more success in overthrowing another than any transformation of its presumed material foundation. The ideology underlying the "theologies" of religion is thus more subtle and destructive than an open atheism, regardless of the pluralists' protestations to the contrary. In terms of intellectual history, the link with English Deism, whose notions of the *religio naturalis* and *theologia naturalis* were the fodder for the atheism of the masses, demonstrates our claim with sufficient eloquence. Therefore the task of comprehensive reflection on interreligious dialogue remains before us in all its cogency, importance, and value.

c. The pluralistic theologies of religion are fragmentary theories of relationality that lack an epistemology that would account for interpersonality and communionality. Just as the Cambridge Platonists and the freethinkers had no doctrine of knowledge that would enable them to differentiate between scientific, moral, and religious knowledge, the theologies of pluralism are plagued by a constant epistemological monism. This monism blocks access to the specificity of truth and of the religions. Truth bears an indelible personalistic and communional stamp that, if adequately obeyed, prevents any lapse into experientialistic, spiritualistic, or

101

religious transcendentalism. The elimination of the subject of truth on the pretext of its inconvenience does not open access to such a logic of communion. This problem becomes even more serious when we consider that religious knowledge itself belongs to the order of interpersonal knowing. It is clear that the absence of an explicit account of such knowledge dooms reflection on religion to superficiality. A glance at the pluralist construal of subjective elements such as experience, feeling, mysticism, or of objective ones such as creation, revelation, divine communication, and redemption, confirms the thinness of the pluralists' understanding of "relation." The impersonality of the relationship with God or with the Ultimate Reality extends, correlatively, to the impersonal way the pluralists conceive and envisage the encounter and relationship among religions. Interreligious dialogue by its very nature needs the accompaniment of a rigorous reflection on relationality.

d. One of the characteristic features that at first sight lends an aura of credibility to the theologies of pluralism is their proclaimed universality. But what kind of universality are we talking about, and even more radically, how ought we to conceive plurality and universality in the first place?

Historically, the modern discussion of the question goes back at least to the seventeenth century when certain authors used the category of universality to unmask the partiality of the Christian religion, which professed to be just that, universal. Christianity proved unable to stand the test of the new geographic globalism that now included a number of new religions. Taking the world's religious geography as the horizon of universality, such authors assumed that Christianity ought to be explained in terms of some larger framework, and not vice versa.

Here universality is understood abstractly as a general quality of a homogeneous series of individual cases, the name of the series being "religion." It is clear that the legitimacy of this abstract approach, with its markedly idealistic flavor, is hardly beyond question.

Another type of universality that supposedly robbed Christianity of its unique place in the mass of religions is a historical one. There is a historical globalism that, taken as a whole, relativizes Christianity. This type of universality assumes temporal sequence as the ultimate explanatory horizon that supposedly undermines Christianity's claimed absoluteness, because it is preceded by other older religions and might evolve toward forms of religion different from those currently in vogue. The genealogy of Christianity secures its relativization, while at the same time setting up an alternative universality that is supposed to be historical or, indeed, "natural."

A third universalistic argument that the pluralists borrow from the seventeenth century is soteriological. A just God cannot *not* desire the salvation of all mankind, but the absoluteness and universality claimed by Christianity do not jibe with such large-mindedness. Here a soteriological egalitarianism determines the conception of universality.

The characters of these three types of universality, each of which possesses a corresponding model of plurality, do not seem adequate either to describe or to justify the unity of the human family and of the different religions of the world. By insisting on common belonging to cosmos, history, and desire for salvation, the pluralists ignore other aspects equally, indeed, even more profoundly, more rooted in the nature of man because placed in him by his Creator and Redeemer. In particular, they are unable to safeguard the integrity of personhood, the communion of persons, and the proper link between the two. But a universality unable to do so is not yet sufficiently universal, and therefore its claims to universality necessarily lead to totalitarianism precisely on the basis of its original egalitarianism, which in this case is a religious egalitarianism.

The Crux of the Pluralists

There Is Only One God —
Is There Only One Mediator?

MICHAEL SCHULZ

Perry Schmidt-Leukel on the Concerns
and Claims of the Pluralistic Theology of Religions

Human beings are living together on a global scale, partly on account of various movements of mass migration. This situation has created new venues for encounter among humanity's religions. The pluralistic theology of religions (= PTR) belongs in this epochal historical context. Its program has been summarized by one of its representatives, the Catholic theologian Perry Schmidt-Leukel, in the essay "Was will die pluralistische Religionstheologie?" ("What Is the Point of the Pluralistic Theology of Religions?").[1] Schmidt-Leukel's purpose is to make this theology better known and to defend it against possible misinterpretations. A personal reading will convey an idea of the controversial theology of religions that Schmidt-Leukel proposes. The critique developed in the following pages refers exclusively to this essay. By focusing on this one text, I hope to make the discussion easier to follow.

According to Schmidt-Leukel, the PTR claims to have succeeded in developing a Christian theory that underwrites an appreciation for the

---

1. Perry Schmidt-Leukel, "Was will die pluralistische Religionstheologie?" *Münchener theologische Zeitschrift* 49 (1998): 307-34. Parenthetical page numbers in the following text refer to this work.

mediations of salvation professed by other religions, an appreciation that goes beyond mere tolerance (315ff.) yet does not substantially affect Christology or the doctrine on God (333).

The PTR claims that whatever saving value is found in other religions comes from God, or rather, God's saving will: "God himself in his universal salvific will and in his self-communication through grace, which Tradition calls the Logos-Christ, is the sole mediator of salvation!" "God himself in his self-opening" is equated with the all-inclusive love of God and with the Logos, who, according to the traditional Christian account, fills the cosmos and "is not simply coincident with the historical Jesus." Otherwise, there could have been no saving love of God and of neighbor before the historical appearance of Jesus (326f.). God's saving action touches history, not only in a small portion of history, but in its entirety (331).

Since, according to the PTR, the Logos and the Jesus of history are not simply the same, there being more than only one point of intersection between God and man (John Hick), the one mediation of God's love or Logos for each individual can take shape in a multiplicity of historical persons. Jesus becomes the mediator of salvation for those who lay hold of him as the appearing of the love of God the savior and in this way are led to overcome their self-centeredness and to live out true love of God and of neighbor (324ff.). Jesus is the event of incarnation as believed by Christians, in other words, the reflection of the universal presence of the absolute Reality (God) in human form that Christians happen to accept. In this account of the incarnation John Hick, the cofounder of the PTR who is particularly esteemed by Schmidt-Leukel (333f.), explains the Christian message of the incarnation of God in terms of a religious pluralism. Later incarnations are not to be ruled out; they can also be believed by other religions.

Aquinas's Christology, says Schmidt-Leukel, seems to support the claim that there can be other incarnations of the love of God that embraces all human beings. Because the creature cannot comprehend and represent the uncreated, there can be an infinite number of mediations and communications of salvation (321).

According to the PTR, the all-inclusiveness of absolute reality finds expression in negative theology — whether Christian, non-Christian, or even philosophical (328-31).

The PTR is described in scientific terms as a "hypothesis." So, too, are the exclusivist and inclusivist accounts of the relationship between Christianity and the other religions. These alternatives to pluralism claim, respectively, that salvation can be found only in Christianity and that salvation comes by way of an implicit ordination to Christ and Christianity (311f., 314f.).

The following critique is as fragmentary as this brief summary — indeed, as the essay of Schmidt-Leukel that sums up the hypothesis of the PTR. Given this brevity, we cannot take into account the varieties of the PTR. Nor can we focus on the varieties of exclusivism and inclusivism, which are by no means monolithic. There is much overlapping and mingling of these three basic approaches. Other approaches within the theology of religions challenge this three-way classification (which, according to Schmidt-Leukel, is "exclusive": 312).[2] The following pages discuss only Schmidt-Leukel's summary of the PTR. We leave aside the question of whether the PTR fosters an appreciation of other religions. It is the adherents of these religions who are most competent to answer this question. What is to be examined and discussed is whether the form of PTR presented by Schmidt-Leukel conveys an appreciation of Christianity, in particular, an appreciation of its underlying philosophy of religion and theory of revelation, which, until now independently of the PTR, have been adopted as the basis for a dialogue with other religions, above all with Judaism and Islam.

Who Is the Mediator?

Immediately striking is the hypothesis that God himself in his self-opening (Logos) is all-embracing love and that in his universal salvific will he is the only mediator of salvation. As the term "*mediator* of salvation" indicates, however, Christianity envisages a mediation *between* God *and* humanity, an unsurpassable point of intersection and unity between the divine and the human. The mediator must embrace and represent *in a perfect way* the two parties whose communication he has to establish. God is the sole origin of salvation. But this salvation becomes relevant to *all* of history only when it enters completely into humanity, indeed, becomes, without any abbreviation, coincident with Jesus. This man, this human will, free of the

2. See instead R. Schenk, "Keine '*unica vera religio*,'" in *Wahrheit*, ed. T. Eggensperge and U. Engle (Mainz, 1993), 167-85.

enfeeblement of sin, of the need for redemption, makes his own God's will to save *all men* who are prisoners of sin and embodies it in a life lived for God and neighbor.

God "desires all men to be saved and to come to the knowledge of the truth. For there is *one* God, and there is one *mediator* between God *and* man, the *man* (!) Christ Jesus, who gave himself as a ransom for all" (1 Tim. 2:4-6). This classic testimony to God's will to save all human beings also attests to the *constitutive* connection between this will and its mediator. This mediator is not simply God; he is not even merely a (gnostic) Christ-Logos; he is not merely the love of God. He is a man: Jesus of Nazareth. According to John, Jesus is the one incarnation of the eternal, coequal divine Logos (John 1). In the Christian understanding, this Logos is the Wisdom of God that brings eschatological salvation. This Wisdom is made manifest in creation and in the history of Israel because (not: although) he is hypostatically united to the man from Nazareth and because he freely realizes God's saving will for all men in an eschatological, definitive, and unsurpassable way. Only an incarnate Logos who brings into existence his own human nature (only thus is he Christ), anointed and consecrated by the Holy Spirit, who unites it to himself in person, and who remains eternally united to it — only he is also the Logos-*Christ* who works salvation for all people and in all times.

Karl Rahner therefore speaks of the singular event of Christ as the *final cause* of God's universal saving will.[3] It is not as man that Jesus plays this causal role. No man can manipulate God. And even before the appearance of Jesus God wills to save all. But this will to save all is real and therefore efficacious for all men only when it is accepted by Jesus without any reduction. The reality of God's will to save includes his divine origin and his human end, both the arrival and the acceptance of this will. As the Son of God, and in his role as unique divine and human mediator, Jesus has performed this acceptance on behalf of all.

Using the language of Rahner, whose understanding of revelation Schmidt-Leukel wishes to harmonize with the PTR, we can formulate this state of affairs in the following way: transcendental revelation (which is general, is addressed to every man, and determines him from within) and categorial revelation (which is concrete and historical) are *two* sides of the one reality of salvation. We cannot play off either of them against the

3. K. Rahner, *Grundkurs des Glaubens* (Freiburg, 1976), 195, 273, 309.

other.[4] In Jesus' history, transcendental revelation reaches its categorially unsurpassable apex; indeed, it is real only insofar as it does so. According to Rahner, the other religions represent a historicity that, however close it comes to the fullness of transcendental revelation, never exhausts it and therefore cannot be considered its decisive final cause.

In an authentic Christian self-understanding, every human being is therefore meant to come to the knowledge of this truth that there is one God and one mediator of salvation for all, the man Jesus Christ. The PTR seems not to be on a level with the Christian understanding of salvation. Its account of soteriology pays insufficient attention to the universal saving import of Jesus' humanity, subscribing instead to a sort of Monophysite or Monothelite identification of the mediator of salvation with God alone, or else neglecting the categorial aspect of God's self-revelation in favor of the transcendental. The decisive point of soteriology stands or falls with the Chalcedonian confession of both the undiminished humanity of Jesus, which includes Jesus' human will, and the undiminished divinity of the incarnate Logos, who bears this humanity and is intimately united with it.

The universal saving significance of the man and Messiah Jesus is expressed in his earthly life in the fact that he brings to pass the eschatologically definitive kingdom of God, his Abba Father (Mark 1:15; Matt. 12:28; Luke 11:20). The quality of one's relation to Jesus decides the quality of one's relation to the kingdom of the God who saves: "everyone who acknowledges me before men, the Son of man will also acknowledge before the angels of God" (Luke 12:8). According to exegetes such as Joachim Gnilka, Jesus — unlike other prophets — decisively links man's eschatological destiny to profession of faith in him.[5]

In all this we can leave open, with Bultmann, the question of whether Jesus is the Son of Man (according to the secondary redaction of the Q logion in Matt. 10:32, Jesus is the Son of Man). 1 Timothy 2:4-6 uses Jesus' death and resurrection to unfold his self-understanding and salvific claim in soteriological and christological terms. Given Jesus' preaching, there can be no question that profession of faith in him includes a praxis of life. It is

---

4. Rahner, *Grundkurs des Glaubens*, 156-65.

5. J. Gnilka, *Das Matthäusevangelium* (Freiburg, 1986), 289ff.; Gnilka, *Jesus von Nazareth* (Freiburg, 1990), 141-65, 261-64; F. Bovon, *Das Evangelium nach Lukas*, Evangelisch-katholischer Kommentar zum Neuen Testament, III/2 (Zürich, 1996), 257ff.; U. Luz, *Das Evangelium nach Matthäus*, Evangelisch-katholischer Kommentar zum Neuen Testament, I/2 (Zürich, 1990), 129ff.; H. Schürmann, *Gottes Reich — Jesu Geschick* (Freiburg, 1983), 143.

equally clear that this profession of faith can be implicit (Luke 9:50). Rigorous historical-critical exegesis shows — perhaps more so than in the past — that Jesus (implicitly) makes a claim to be the eschatological mediator of salvation. It also brings to light the development of the confession that reflects this claim. Schmidt-Leukel is misleading when he asserts (321f.) that most recent exegesis tells against the church's christological dogma. There are equally many studies of the history of dogma that demonstrate the inner continuity of the development of this dogma.[6]

Schmidt-Leukel, invoking Pannenberg's Christology (323), insists on the theocentrism of Jesus' preaching of the kingdom of God (321ff.). Yet Jesus' theocentrism is a far cry from the relativization of Jesus as the sole savior or of his divine authority. According to Pannenberg, in fact, the correlate of Jesus' theocentrism is the filiocentrism of the Father, who reveals the divinity of the Son in their common Spirit.[7] This very theocentrism is what underscores the perfect realization of Jesus' humanity vis-à-vis God. These two aspects of Jesus' theocentrism are inseparable.

One has the impression that Schmidt-Leukel is concerned to weaken the christological underpinnings of soteriology in order to be able to demonstrate more easily the compatibility of the PTR with Christianity. It should be noted that this program has enjoyed a certain, albeit not general or even dominant, popularity, not only among the contemporaries of Reimarus or Strauss but also in the present. John Hick and others interpret the statements of individual theologians one-sidedly or selectively in order to claim Christian theological support for the pluralistic interpretation of Christianity.[8]

It is, then, an abuse to cite Pannenberg's thoroughly trinitarian theology or his theology of religions in order to undermine Christianity. To use

6. See, for example, W. Thüsing, *Die neutestamentlichen Theologien und Jesus Christus,* vol. 1 (Munich, 1996), 65-96, 141-43, 156-70, 262-68; vol. 2 (Munich, 1998), 160-85; K. Berger, *Theologiegeschichte des Urchristentums* (Tübingen, 1994), 19-24, 55-63, 103-5, 224-33, 277f.; R. Schnackenburg, *Die Person Jesu Christi im Spiegel der vier Evangelien,* Herder theologischer Kommentar zum Neuen Testament — Supplementband 4 (Freiburg, 1993), 58-66, 327-54; Gnilka, *Jesus von Nazareth,* 86-165; Gnilka, *Theologie des Neuen Testaments,* Herder theologischer Kommentar zum Neuen Testament — Supplementband 5 (Freiburg, 1994), 13-140, 146ff., 159-65, 188ff., 205-10, 234-39, 246-86, 294-302, 326-33, 368-85, 454f.; A. Grillmeier, *Jesus der Christus im Glauben der Kirche,* vol. 1 (Freiburg, 1979); P. Hünermann, *Jesus der Christus. Gottes Wort in der Zeit* (Paderborn, 1994), 66-192. This list could easily be lengthened.

7. Cf. W. Pannenberg, *Systematische Theologie,* vol. 1 (Göttingen, 1988), 337; vol. 2 (Göttingen, 1991), 413f.

8. See Schenk, 174ff.

Michael Schulz

Pannenberg's Christology as a source for the theological grounding of the PTR is an injustice. There are also many Catholic systematicians who, while hardly "right-wingers," nonetheless express their disappointment with the pluralists' deconstruction of soteriological and christological dogma.[9]

Neglect of the one, exclusive mediation of salvation performed by the *man* Jesus Christ as Son *of God* and disregard of Christ's human freedom are consistent with the attempt to undermine christological dogma. Only a weakening of the exclusive link between God's will to save all and its final cause, the event of Christ, can lend plausibility to the claim that there are other, *autonomous* human mediations of salvation. The saving value of such mediations thus no longer needs to be grounded in some implicit relation to the savior, Jesus, who is intrinsic to God's will to save all men. All that is required is an abstract, suprahistorical relation with the love of God in his desire to save.

On the other hand, to the extent that it wishes to argue from a Christian point of view, the PTR is obliged to base its knowledge of God's universal saving will on the event of Christ. In fact, God's freedom forbids any philosophical deduction of the reality of salvation; if we follow Blondel, we must say that a philosophy of religion can at best glimpse the possibility of salvation from afar. We can therefore speak of a *real* universal salvation only in view of the historical event of salvation in Christ envisaged by 1 Timothy 2:5-6. By the same token we cannot act like Monophysites in reducing the exclusive mediation of salvation to God, or to the divine love, while proposing a hyper-Antiochene detachment of salvation from an exclusive human and historical mediation. Nor must we succumb to a postmodern limitation of Christian salvation to historical Christendom.

The PTR is heavily indebted to Lessing: the Absolute cannot become an event of universal salvation while remaining *consistent with itself and its uniqueness,* which is to say, in an unsurpassable, definitive, and unique — or in biblical terms eschatological-historical — way. In view of the eschatological character of Jesus' proclamation and praxis of the kingdom of God, which he enacts in a singular way in his death and resurrection, Pannenberg is surely right to speak of this death and resurrection as an an-

9. See, for example, K.-J. Kuschel, "Christologie und Pluralistische Religionstheologie," in *Wege der Theologie,* ed. G. Risse (Paderborn, 1996), 481-93; H. Waldenfels, "Theologie der Religionen," *Stimmen der Zeit* 123 (1998): 291-301, esp. 296f.

ticipation, or prolepsis, of God's absolute future, or as a singular, unsurpassable presence of the Absolute in history — as a presence that relativizes all other religions (in the twofold meaning of the word "relativize").[10]

The concrete, objective, and unsurpassable presence of the Absolute for all in Jesus' history is foreign to the PTR. The PTR merely restates in soteriological terms Lessing's well-known dictum concerning the ugly, unbridgeable ditch between the subjective, regional truths of history — the "perishable facts" — and the truths of reason, which, Lessing says, can rightly claim suprahistorical validity. Any philosophy or theology of religion that would remain in the center of Christianity must do the opposite, namely, show how the Absolute can be the event of salvation for all men in a historical, objectively unsurpassable singularity.

The Party Is Always Right — and the Christ of Christianity?

In the former East Germany a communist party slogan claimed that "the party is always right." Christianity's claim to absoluteness sounds similar — at least to some. Christians, however, do not conceive themselves to be a group of human beings who have decided to claim superiority for their own religion. Jesus claims to bring about the salvation of all men in history. It is by virtue of this claim that Christians profess their faith in the absoluteness of Jesus, an absoluteness, they believe, manifested in his unity with God both in being and in action.

One might accuse Jesus of megalomania and then lay the same charge at the feet of his disciples. The response to this objection requires a philosophy of religion and a theory of revelation. It requires arguments explaining that and how God's definitive revelation can occur as an event in the history of a single human being. Such arguments must show that it is not a priori absurd to claim, as Christians do, that a single human being is in fact that definitive revelation of God. To conduct one's argument below this threshold is, to put it bluntly, a waste of time; it affords no opportunity to develop a theory that has any pertinence to Christ and Christianity.

---

10. W. Pannenberg, *Offenbarung als Geschichte* (Göttingen, 1982), 105f.; Pannenberg, *Grundfragen systematischer Theologie* (Göttingen, 1979), 43ff., 60ff., 66-78; Pannenberg, *Systematische Theologie*, 1:167-88, 207f., 215ff., 231, 250f., 270-81.

By the same token the philosophy of religion must adopt the concrete fact of Christ as its starting point. A concept of religion built (in typically Enlightenment fashion) solely upon man's theoretical or practical reason has an innate tendency to reduce Christianity, and in general any historical religion, to a function of the enlightening work of a supposedly "rational religion."

On the other hand, the fact that every school of thought — even a philosophy or theology of religion — always has a particular standpoint is not an unfortunate disadvantage that threatens its objectivity and universal validity. For the PTR the presupposition of standpoints seems, at best, a necessary evil. In reality, having reference points is constitutive of the human spirit, which as both Aquinas and Rahner tell us, can be present neither to itself nor to the truth of the other without a *conversio ad phantasma*, without a relation to the sensible and visible, the concrete and historical. Without a concrete standpoint of our own we cannot reach anyone else's. Man, being finite, can never radically disjoin the *validity* of a truth from its origin in a historical situation, which is always tied to a point of view; the visible plays a role even in the most abstract thinking (Thomas Aquinas, *Summa theologiae* [hereafter *ST*] 1.84.7).[11]

A theory of revelation and a philosophy of religion come to maturity within the christological and trinitarian center of Christianity are able both to give an account of Christianity and to dialogue with the assumptions underlying the truth claims of other religions. Only such an account, it would seem, can avoid the danger that, say, a Muslim who examines the PTR might find the philosophy of religion it presupposes to be a typical product of the Western Enlightenment that a priori relativizes the truth claim of his own religion in order to make room for a mutual tolerance and respect on peripheral questions having nothing to do with the now empty center of concern.

Certainly the PTR does not *intend* to empty out the center of any religion in order to ground respect for it. It remains to be seen, however, whether the PTR has the intellectual resources to make good on its intention — in terms not only of soteriology and Christology, but also, as we will examine and illustrate below, of the doctrine of God.

Transcendental theology's reflection on the definitiveness and unsurpassability of the revelation of God in Jesus shows that these quali-

11. K. Rahner, *Geist in Welt* 1939 (Sonderausgabe, 1996), 69-83.

ties have to do with profession of faith in the *divinity* of the word of revelation. In Jesus, God must truly have acted *as himself,* since only God or his unique historical presence is *unsurpassable;* only this presence can be something definitive within time. If in Jesus Christ God had merely produced some *created* grace (a miracle, a healing, the forgiveness of individual sins, the communication of messages tailored to specific situations), then his action in Jesus would not have been definitive. A creature can always be surpassed. For the same reason a *created* Logos could not be the mediator of a definitive revelation of *God.* Only the uncreated status of the Logos can guarantee the inner coherence of Peter's profession of faith in the Acts of the Apostles: "and there is salvation in no one else" (4:12). On this basis the theology of the Trinity makes explicit the ultimate reason or the definitiveness of salvation in Christ.

It is no accident, therefore, that despite its partiality to a strict negative theology, Islam has insisted on the eternity of the divine, uncreated word of revelation that is rendered by the Koran (as a written text). The ninth-century Mutazilites attempted to bring home the unbridgeable difference between the uncreated God and the created world; they argued that the Koran was created. Significantly, this theory failed to persuade the Muslim world.[12] This failure reinforced the Islamic conviction that Muhammad is the "seal of the prophets"; only the communication of the *divine* word is unsurpassable. Of course, Islam has refused the trinitarian implication that Christians have found necessary: "In the beginning was the Word, and the Word was God." Interestingly, the Mutazilites were sworn foes of this theology of the Logos.[13]

The Old Testament leaves open the question concerning the status of the mediators through whom God acts in Israel's history: Are the word and the spirit created or uncreated? The Wisdom literature nevertheless clearly shows the tendency to accord Wisdom, though still regarded as a creature, a special position with respect to the rest of the world. It thus acquires an obvious claim to be the privileged means of the revelation of the uncreated God.

We must insist, then, that the profession of faith in the definitiveness of the revelation of God in Jesus depends on the unsurpassable divinity of the word of revelation made manifest in him. This suggests the following

12. T. Nagel, *Der Koran* (Munich, 1991), 336ff.
13. J. Boumann, *Gott und Mensch im Koran* (Darmstadt, 1989), 61f.

method for dealing with the possibility of, say, another religion for which the claim to the absolute truth of a historical singularity was also central. In light of Christianity, we would have to make the argument that this central claim must include belief in the undiminished divinity of what this religion presents as a manifestation of God in history — for example, a word of revelation. Moreover, if this hypothetical religion should prove to link divinity with historical singularity in this way, we would then have to bring into play further reflections concerning the assumptions and conditions of this unsurpassable unity of an absolute message and a human messenger (see below).

The PTR seems to share the first idea of the theory of revelation when it speaks of the Logos of *God*, who savingly permeates the universe and the history of humanity. This idea is obscured insofar as it overlooks the knowledge of God that is necessary to secure the plausibility of this proposal.

The Night in Which All Cows Are Black

Invoking the negative theology common both to Christianity and to other traditions, the PTR unhesitatingly declares that the various "names, titles, images, and concepts" of transcendent reality are "in principle equally valid" (329). Unfortunately, this avowal makes it impossible to relativize Neoplatonic accounts of negative theology that exclude even an internal differentiation of knower and known from the unity of the absolute one. This is unfortunate because faith in God's self-revelation presupposes a God capable of making himself known on the basis of his own self-knowledge. The *Christian* character of negative theology depends on the possibility of these sorts of differentiations. It is thus in the interest of the Christian doctrine of God to show philosophically that an entity that can know itself is superior to one that cannot.[14]

Once this is granted, we can readily understand the argument that the Absolute necessarily comprehends itself, even though we cannot state univocally just how there is real self-knowledge in God. One thing, however, is clear: God's self-knowing is infinitely more intense than ours.

The PTR's talk about God's revelatory Logos, taken at face value, assumes God's capacity to express himself entirely in the Logos/Word; it as-

---

14. L. Elders, *Die Metaphysik des Thomas von Aquin*, vol. 2 (1987), 223f.

sumes a divine self-knowledge. Insofar as the PTR aims to valorize Christianity, it must establish a philosophical knowledge of God that can account for his self-opening from within. Otherwise the concept of God's self-disclosure takes on a completely different meaning, so that it no longer makes sense to clarify what it is in God that allows him to disclose himself; everything gives way to a radicalized negative theology. Conversely, philosophical reflection on God's self-knowledge (and on the other divine properties) guarantees the communicability of the presuppositions of the Christian faith in revelation, and therefore secures a knowledge of God that has bearing on salvation even on the level of theoretical reason. It enables us to explain these presuppositions to a non-Christian interlocutor who accepts this paradigm of reason. This method exploits the Christian concept of revelation.

If, then, the PTR obliges us to speak of the incomprehensibility of God, the Christian cannot understand this incomprehensibility after the fashion of the absolute identity that Hegel perceives in Schelling's philosophy. According to Hegel, Schelling holds that the Absolute makes itself known as the "night in which, as they say, all cows are black." Hegel bluntly calls the statement that in the Absolute everything is somehow the same as everything else "the naiveté of the void of knowledge."[15]

In order to avoid this naiveté, the representatives of negative theology within Christianity whom Schmidt-Leukel cites — for example, Thomas Aquinas — are concerned to link their negative theology to an analogical thinking that enables them to formulate analogously true statements regarding God's being (Aquinas, *ST* 1.13.3). The contents signified by such statements do not merge in a total indistinction on account of the divine unity; the perfections drawn from the finite and predicated analogically of God preexist in that unity (1.13.4).

Without analogical knowledge of God, the "divine incomprehensibility" ends up being just a pious metaphor for atheism, to which, of course, the PTR does not intend to give theoretical aid and comfort. On this point the PTR intends to be decidedly exclusivistic (Schmidt-Leukel, 312). Western thought offers a sure means for drawing the line between belief and atheism: reference to God's being, not only as nonfinite but also, positively, as a pure reality that knows and wills itself (Aquinas, *ST* 1.14.1-14). Accord-

15. G. W. F. Hegel, *Phänomenologie des Geistes. Werkausgabe,* ed. E. Moldenhauer and K. M. Michel (Frankfurt, 1970), 22.

ing to Aquinas, "being" is the most adequate name for God, since it does not contain any delimitation (1.13.11). Admitting the predication of being, we can make "adequate" affirmative-analogical statements about God (1.13.12). Because "being" and the other perfections said to belong to God can never be truly unlimited in finite things, the finite can never serve as a springboard for univocal statements about the divine being (1.13.12).

According to Thomas, man does not stand before God as before an unattainable object inaccessible to human knowledge. Thomas recognizes that God's light exceeds man, yet he does not conclude from this either that man cannot know God or that there is no eschatological vision of him. In his commentary on the *Metaphysics,* Aquinas rejects as inadequate Aristotle's comparison of man to a bat accustomed to the dark of night that is suddenly blinded by the clear light of day.[16] In *Summa theologiae* Thomas connects the example of the bat with the argument that given the plenitude of God's all-illuminating light, the created intellect is incapable of seeing God. In contrast, Thomas emphasizes that the human spirit is capable of ascending to the original cause of every being; otherwise man could never reach his perfection (1.12.1). A human being who exhaustedly and vainly sought the first case is for Aquinas a monstrosity contrary to nature. Thomas rules out only a univocal grasping or comprehending of God by the created intellect.

Aquinas's negative theology is thus foreign to an extreme Neoplatonic metaphysics of the unknowable One beyond the categories of identity and difference (1.12.1-3).[17] Insofar as Christian thinkers and mystics approach a negative theology that removes all affirmative predication and distinction from God, they are liable to critique. By the same token it would also be incorrect to transform the mysticism of different religions and its often negative concept of God into a metareligion of an ungraspable, undifferentiated divine One. We must rather attend to the context that shapes the particular form of mysticism in question.[18]

16. See Elders, 191.

17. H. U. von Balthasar, *Theologik,* vol. 2 (Einsiedeln, 1985), 98: "If 'silence' stands at the end of negative philosophical theology because the darts of all concepts and words fall to the ground before finding their mark, a different silence stands at the end of Christian theology: that of adoration, which is likewise struck dumb by reason of the exceeding measure of the gift given."

18. H. Bürkle, *Der Mensch auf der Suche nach Gott — die Frage der Religionen* (Paderborn, 1996), 218-21.

Analogy also gives Aquinas the confidence to infer the possibility of two intradivine processions, not in order to "prove" the Trinity philosophically but to demonstrate that it is not at all contradictory to maintain two processions within God, even as the existence of these processions must be accepted on the basis of revelation (1.27).

According to Anselm, to whom Schmidt-Leukel appeals as an exponent of negative theology, philosophical knowledge of God is fulfilled in the demonstration of the Trinity. He shows philosophically that God is that than which nothing greater can be thought, indeed, that God is ever greater than anything we can conceive, that he is the source of every finite good, and consequently that he is eminently entitled to be identified with the Good that is worthy of all desire. Anselm also demonstrates the procession of the eternal Word: in this Word the God who is always greater and who knows himself expresses himself in a unique, singular way. Through this Word he both creates and reveals himself. According to Anselm, we cannot know God and the Trinity immediately, but only through the mediation of the creature, through the openness of the human spirit to the ineffable divinity, and through its likeness to God.[19]

Christianity has developed a negative theology not simply because the human intellect finds it difficult to know God, but rather because of the superabundance of God's revelation, whose communication to man requires an ultimate personal engagement on man's part. The more present an entity is to itself (hence, the more it is a subject), the more personal commitment is required to grasp it. The knowledge of a stone does not require much commitment; the knowledge of a man requires incomparably more.

Compared to the knowledge of objects, the knowledge of personal being is more difficult; something that cannot be grasped opens itself. But this knowledge is not more imprecise on this account. It is an opening up of the other's capacity for self-revelation, an opening that demands the entire being of the knower.

If the other's intensity of being is infinite, the process of knowledge is also infinite. This infinity of knowledge certainly does not imply the futility of the endeavor to grasp and embrace, but rather expresses the inexhaustible "always more" that manifests itself in an unlimited attraction that invites us to go on knowing the other, or as the case may be, God, "al-

---

19. Anselm of Canterbury, *Proslogion* 2, 15; Anselm, *Monologion* 1ff., 12, 30ff., 65ff.

ways more." The negative aspect of knowing is a function of the perception of a positive "ever greater" fullness of truth, so that — especially in relation to God — there is no brake, no obligation to remain fixed on a certain level of knowledge *(via negationis)*. There is always "more" to know (the *via affirmationis* as a *via eminentiae*). The knowledge of God is possible because his being is "always more"; it possesses a superabundant determinacy. This knowledge does not plunge into a dark abyss or an undifferentiated absolute unity; it becomes ever more differentiated and ever more conformed to the limitlessness of the horizon of human knowing; it becomes ever more fulfilling. Thus, according to Thomas, the revelation of the Trinity frees us from certain errors *(ST* 1.1.1), guarantees a better understanding of the freedom of creation (1.32.1, 3), and reveals God as the foundation of all knowledge, a foundation that can be grasped precisely as ungraspable. Only because this comprehensive personal knowledge has no end can the human spirit, finite and yet open to the infinite, reach its goal and its peace in the vision of God, into which it penetrates ever more deeply (in an atemporal fashion).

The PTR is inadequate insofar as it does not expressly secure God's elusiveness and inexhaustible knowability on the metaphysical basis of his personal nature. In order to preserve the positive elusiveness of God, we must not reduce this personal character to the level of an undifferentiated absolute.

The negative theology of a Thomas Aquinas would also be turned on its head if we considered the personality of God only as a further, secondary manifestation of the essentially unknowable divine reality that underlies all such manifestations. There is no conceivably denser unity than the incommunicable self-presence of the person. The PTR's concept of the Absolute must do justice to these basic features of the Christian doctrine of God; otherwise it would alienate Christianity from itself and would end up with a nominally Christian vocabulary concealing what is in fact another religion.

Drawing on its own central convictions, and out of a desire for dialogue, especially with other religions that claim a revelation, Christianity must attempt to give a philosophical account of God's personhood. It is notoriously difficult to work with the concept of person in the dialogue with the Asian religions, because (as also happens in Fichte's philosophy) they often fix it in the sphere of the finite. We cannot evade these difficulties by remaining silent about the reality indicated by the concept of divine (and, therefore, human) "person" or by treating Christian (as well as Jewish and Muslim) talk about the personal God as somehow secondary.[20]

As we have seen, the understanding of revelation as the *self-communication* of God depends on the analogical attribution of personhood to God. According to the Christian faith, God's self-communication cannot be adequately understood as a quantifiable mass of information. If we assumed an information theory of revelation, it would, of course, be quite logical to speak of many equally valid revelations. We could collect all the bits of information made known in the various religions in order to work out a superconcept of the essence of what God has informed us of. This concept would thus contain quantitatively "more" revelation about God than any particular religion — which would certainly put the religions in a difficult position. But since God is not quantifiable, neither is his self-communication. What is revealed is always the one and only God; his revelation, however, reaches its summit where he himself becomes historically present as himself, and not merely by way of created signs (see below).

In order, therefore, to speak of a definitive revelation of God in history, we need to be able to develop a philosophy of religion that demonstrates God's existence, unity, self-knowledge and freedom, and therefore his personhood. Rahner's *Hörer des Wortes* is a classic example of such a philosophy of religion. It would be impossible, at least in principle, to formulate the underlying presuppositions of Christianity in a more abstract and philosophical way — at the risk, that is, of thinking outside identifiably Christian faith.

Thomas and the Multiplicity of Incarnations

Schmidt-Leukel uses Thomas's Christology (321) in support of his claim of the possibility of a multiplicity of incarnations and mediations of salvation. According to this argument, the uncreated cannot be comprehended by the created (*"non comprehendi potest"*: ST 3.3.7). We can observe in passing that this reasoning illustrates the problem of the knowledge of

20. On the hermeneutics of understanding governing the dialogue between religions, see Bürkle, 226-40.

God (Schmidt-Leukel, 329). In fact, God's unknowability can be accounted for in very different, even opposite ways.

First of all, we need to ascertain Thomas's own intention. He advances this argument in order to clarify that the *power* of a divine person is not limited or exhausted by the creature. It is thus theoretically possible for a divine person to assume more than one human nature. Saint Thomas asks similar questions about the Father and the Holy Spirit — could they, in principle, have become man (*ST* 3.3.5, 8)? — and indeed, about the divine nature itself — could the divine nature have assumed a human nature (3.3)?

Using this and other hypothetical constructs, Thomas attempts to demonstrate God's infinite power and freedom with respect to the creature. God could have accomplished the redemption of humanity otherwise than he in fact did. Nevertheless, Aquinas's intention is not to construct an arbitrary God who simply decided thus and who could at any moment act in a completely different manner if he so chose. A doctrine that gives such priority to the *potentia Dei absoluta* that it threatens the link between God's being and revelation, thus reductively foreshortening the reality of the saving order to the positive decree of the divine will, is alien to Thomas's thinking. Thus, having highlighted the fundamental freedom of God, Aquinas always attempts to evince the reasons of fittingness that display the logic of the real order of salvation and provoke wonder at the wisdom with which God creates and acts in history.

Thomas thus shows that it is supremely fitting — that it corresponds eminently to God's wisdom — that the Son, rather than another divine person (3.3.8), should assume human nature. In precisely the same way he shows that it is human nature, rather than any other, that was most suitably assumed by the Son. The fact that this nature is capable of God — *capax Dei* — and in need of redemption, exposed to the misery of sin, speaks in favor of this claim (4.1).

Thomas's point, then, is that the one historical incarnation is not necessary, and that this nonnecessity reflects the limitless power of the divine Word. A second incarnation is hypothetically possible. But Aquinas would doubtless vigorously protest if he were informed that what he considers a mere logical or intellectual possibility authorized the positive affirmation that other incarnations have already happened in fact. Thomas's aim is to demonstrate precisely the inner coherence of the historically unique order of salvation as Christianity understands it, and to do so in terms of its fittingness. The nonnecessity of this order implies the logical possibility of another — but this logical possibility cannot be secretly transformed into a real possibility (Duns Scotus).

We must emphatically insist on the distinction between logical and real possibility. God's sovereign decision to create or to communicate himself makes all the difference between them. Man's decision to declare a logical possibility a real possibility has no power to do so. The point is that once what has been given has in fact been given, it becomes necessary to clarify its presupposition. The difference between reasons of fittingness and of necessity does not authorize any judgment about alternative realities actually, and not just possibly, ordained by God.

From the hermeneutical point of view, then, it is not possible, without turning Aquinas's own intention completely upside down, to establish the *reality* of another, multiincarnational order of salvation using the arguments from fittingness that Thomas adopts to ground the order actually existing in Christ. The appeal to the unlimitedness of the divine power is not to the point here.

Thomas also explicitly rejects the supposition that the Son of God had to assume human nature in all individual human beings (3.4.5). As an initial argument in favor of this theory, Thomas cites a passage invoked by Schimdt-Leukel. This passage could almost serve as a summary of the program of the PTR as Schmidt-Leukel understands it: "The incarnation of God is a work of the divine love. . . . Nevertheless, love urges the lover to communicate himself to his friends as far as he can. We have shown that it would have been possible for the Son of God to assume more than one human nature [3.7]. Therefore, he could just as well have united himself to all human beings. And so it would have been fitting for the Son of God to assume human nature in all of its supposits."

Thomas refutes this argument by pointing out, among other things, that in the real order of salvation history only *one* divine person in fact became man, so that it was also fitting that this *one* person should assume only *one* human nature: *"ut ex utraque parte unitas inveniatur"* (3.4.5). The PTR does not see this intrinsic ("fitting") link between the divine person of the Logos and the one human nature he assumed, both of which are unique and each of which implies the other. Instead, it looks to other, abstract logical possibilities as an argument for the reality of their presupposition that there is in fact an alternative order of salvation.

This way of thinking presupposes a vantage point from which to survey the whole from above. The need for the intellect's *conversio ad phantasma* in the context of the theory of the incarnation is no longer taken into consideration. In other words, the PTR simply excises any constitutive reference to the concrete incarnation of God in Christ as the foundation of the knowledge of real conditions of possibility. Having climbed up the ladder of the event of Christ to reach a conception of other logical possibilities of incarnation, the PTR kicks the ladder away in order to pass judgment on the reality of the actual incarnation from above.

Moreover, Thomas rules out as metaphysically impossible the idea that God could somehow become incarnate in all human beings, because in so doing God would eliminate the multiplicity of the supposits that sustain and realize human nature. In the end, the person of the Logos would be the sole bearer of a single human nature.

However much Aquinas thus emphasizes the creature's incapacity to limit the action, or to exhaust the incommensurability of God, he does not conclude from this that it would be fitting for the one God or the one Logos to become incarnate in many, or ultimately in all, human beings. Many incarnations would not exhaust the incommensurability of God any more than one. By definition this incommensurability admits of no exhaustive end. If, however, God became incarnate as himself for all men in just one man, inasmuch as the Logos becomes the principle of the existence of a human nature (hypostatic union), then he was indeed able to reveal himself in the created (embracing it, without being embraced by it) — once and for all (Heb. 7:27) — and to give himself as our salvation.

Man is capable of expressing the infinite divinity, despite Schmidt-Leukel's declaration to the contrary, because man is capable of *God* (= *capax Dei*) and because God *wants* to communicate himself within the unlimited spiritual nature of man. If God could not become incarnate *as himself in his incommensurability,* he could not become incarnate *as himself at all.* Lessing would be right.

Once again Thomas's positive concern is to show that the uniqueness of the incarnation was possible both from the human and the divine point of view and that it was fitting in every respect. The PTR cannot legitimately invoke Aquinas to support a multiplicity of incarnations in the sense in which it intends to affirm that multiplicity — without, that is, turning Thomas's position into its precise opposite.

Aquinas and Hegel: The True Absolute's
Unlimited Power to Assume Man

In his philosophy of religion Hegel likewise examines the logical consistency of a supposed plurality of incarnations.[21] The conclusion of this examination is that the assumption of a plurality of incarnations would render the incarnation of God — the divine humanity — abstract: a property that can be abstracted and predicated of many.

If, however, the incarnate divine humanity could be attributed to several supposits, it could no longer be understood as a historically concrete predicate of the one and only absolute subjectivity of God in his self-communication; the predicate would no longer definitively explicate the unique divine subjectivity (in the sense of the *speculative* principle that the subject equals the predicate and vice versa).

Hegel, responding to Lessing and Kant, wants to show that the Absolute can become historical *as itself*, can reveal itself to man, and that it cannot be grasped only on the level of abstract determinations of reason or of general predicates. General predicates are not adequate to the Absolute, which is the master of human history and can manifest itself therein in a unique way.

According to Hegel, the ability to assume man *(capacitas hominis)* is the distinguishing mark of the absoluteness of God: God has power over what is other than himself. Both the divinity of God and the finitude of the finite are preserved, at the level of thought, only if finitude is not made an insurmountable barrier to the possibilities of God's self-manifestation. Otherwise the finite would become absolute in its finitude and, at the same time, God would be limited in his power, thus becoming finite.

We cannot, therefore, apodictically exclude the possibility of a natural knowledge of God. If God is God, he can make himself known to a being that grasps the limited and finite within the horizon of the absolute and infinite. Such a being, in fact, is in principle open to the Absolute. God can even, as we have explained, become incarnate without diminishment in this man who is open to him. To affirm the contrary contradicts the divinity of God and the limitlessness of man even in his finitude.

Hegel therefore exposes the claim that philosophy and theology can-

---

21. Cf. G. W. F. Hegel, *Vorlesungen über die Philosophie der Religion,* vol. 3, ed. Werner Jaeschke (1984), 49; M. Schulz, *Sein und Trinität* (St. Ottilien, 1997), 400-406.

not know God, that there can be no unique incarnation, that God cannot be known in the man-God Jesus Christ, as false modesty, as a dramatic failure of theology. To point, in supposed humility, to the finitude of the human spirit as an argument for the unknowability of God is to absolutize finitude in a pseudoself-sufficiency that runs counter to its fundamental tendency.

And a theology that cannot imagine a unique, unsurpassable self-manifestation of God in history cannot do justice to the true absoluteness of God, which cannot be limited by man. Thus, precisely because, as Thomas says, the uncreated cannot by comprehended by the creature, it is also true that the uncreated can comprehend the creature, indeed, can do so to any extent it wishes, and therefore can present itself *entirely as itself* in the creature. *This* is the ultimate point of Thomas's affirmation — a point that escapes the PTR.

The Messenger and the Message:
The Uniqueness of the Incarnation

A philosophy of religion or theory of revelation can show that an exhaustive self-communication of God presupposes the divinity of this communication; only the uncreated character of this communication constitutes its unsurpassability. But, as we must now show, the unity between the divine message and its human mediator must also be unsurpassable. In the absence of this unity we cannot speak of an absolute revelation in history that corresponds to the absoluteness of God.

A relative unity between God's self-communication and its human mediator can always be surpassed. The series of messengers remains in principle indefinite. If Christianity were regarded as a religion based on the relative unity between the divine word and its human mediation, it could not count as what Hegel calls the "absolute religion." The PTR has to evacuate the core of Christianity in order to establish its own compatibility with that core, but the mere relative unity of word and mediator would have accomplished this goal long ago.

The Christian theory of revelation poses the following question for Islam: How can Muhammad be the "seal of the prophets," and how can a book, the Koran, be the conclusion of revelation? A relative unity between the self-manifestation of God and a prophetic mediator, the categorial presence of the word of revelation in a book, could be surpassed by an absolute unity — by a hypostatic union of God and man. The statements of the Koran to the effect that Jesus is the Word of God naturally do not rise to the level of christological faith.[22]

A human nature that owes its concrete existence to a human person created by God can only be called by God to announce his closeness to man; it cannot, however, be itself the eschatological closeness and self-communication of God in person.

But this is precisely what happens when God himself is the personal bearer, or supposit, and therefore the principle of the existence, of a concrete human nature. It is not therefore God's will to create, but rather his will to communicate himself, that serves as the metaphysical foundation of the existence of Christ's human nature — if this nature is to mediate God's unsurpassable closeness in history. As long as the Word in which God communicates himself is not the immediate personal foundation of the existence of the messenger, we cannot speak of an incarnation or an unsurpassable revelation of God in history.

The idea of an absolute religion, deriving from the philosophy of religion, is the idea of a historical religion of the incarnation of God: of God's hypostatic union with a human nature.[23] This idea must be taken from the center of Christianity and introduced into interreligious dialogue to guide the formulation of criteria for detecting a definitive appearance of God in history.

For Aquinas the hypostatic union of the divine and human natures in virtue of a single bearer of existence, the person of the Logos, is the greatest unity that can be conceived apart from the unity of God (*ST* 3.2.9). For this reason the incarnation occurs only in the supreme form of divine-human unity.

Because the PTR does not define incarnation in terms of hypostatic union, but in a generic way that prescinds from the question of hypostasis, it cannot claim to represent the core of Christian Christology or the Christian account of revelation. Thomas explicitly observes that the unity that comes into being with the incarnation far surpasses numerical unity and that, like the unity of God or of a divine person, it cannot be conceived as an instance or part of some greater unity (3.2.9). The PTR, however, does

22. Boumann, 60f., 67.
23. See Schulz, 860-75.

exactly this: there is a higher unity, and it is the abstract predicate "incarnation."

The PTR's concept of revelation is therefore abstract, that is to say, it is detached from its *constitutive* highest categorial form. It becomes a universal predicate that can be said of many individual instances. The original meaning of terms like "incarnation," "revelation," and "mediation of salvation" is thus inverted into a generic abstraction. The PTR only appears to safeguard the Christian theology of the incarnation. In reality it fails to do so because it does not develop a philosophy of religion capable of serving as a criterion for discerning a definitive revelation. But in order to do justice to Christianity's understanding of itself, a definitive revelation is precisely what one must have.

The PTR'S Forgetfulness of Sin

Schmidt-Leukel thus twists Rahner's statement that the incarnation is the supreme, indeed, unique case of human self-fulfillment in the direction of a generic concept of "incarnation" that can be applied, with differences in degree only, to all, inasmuch as the individual in question more or less intensely realizes his own essence (324f.). The PTR thus blurs the difference between the hypostatic union and the election of man to prophethood. Once he has abusively cited Rahner to justify the reduction of the Christian understanding of the incarnation to mere human flourishing — without any explicit reference to the reality of the one savior — Schmidt-Leukel asks the question that, on these presuppositions, is indeed quite logical: "Would it not perhaps be exceedingly strange if among all human beings only one were to achieve a fully realized human existence?" (324).

Rahner is clear that the one supreme case of human self-fulfillment is given exclusively in Christ. Indeed, Jesus is, as man, without original or personal sin. Because his will is not weakened by any sin, it can let God's will to self-communication shine through, indeed, can assume the totality of this divine will without dilution. Christ does this in solidarity with all human beings, who, because of Adam's free refusal to realize and accept God's desire for self-communication, are no longer able to correspond to God's love, so that human self-fulfillment falls far short, in its deficiency and guilt, of the possibilities that God freely bestows upon it.

The PTR, following the Enlightenment, but contrarily to the theology of the Reformers and the intuitions of "small ecumenism," minimizes the radical threat of sin, a situation that does not allow humanity to become what God had initially intended it to be and, but for the choice of Adam, it could have been.

Admittedly, man can measure the radicality of his exposure to sin only in the light of Christ's redemption, so that a philosophy of religion alone finds it difficult to explain the deficit in which human existence finds itself in spite of the divine will. A Christian philosophy of religion should, however, at least attempt to make a case for the universal need for redemption that in fact exists, even if not caused by God. In the absence of the event of Christ, it is tempting to link this need for redemption to man's limited, finite nature. But to succumb to this temptation would be to set aside the idea of a good Creator. And redemption would be nothing but a "liberation" from the limits of human nature.

Going by Schmidt-Leukel's summary of the PTR, we note that it has little to say about sin and guilt and, therefore, about man's need for redemption. On the contrary, if we follow John Macquarrie, whom Schmidt-Leukel cites, in holding that the incarnation "represents no singularity or anomaly in the history of the world" (325), then our account of the revelation and incarnation of God neglects the problem of sin — which means that we are attempting to prescind from the unique saving action of God who, in Christ, overcomes all sins. But without this action man is doomed never to attain his destined self-fulfillment.

The Crucial Question: Only One for All?

The citation from Macquarrie offers further confirmation of the PTR's inability to perceive Christ as the *universale concretum* of salvation. It thus embraces an anomaly, if the claims of Luke 22:8, 1 Timothy 2:4-6, Acts 4:12, John 14:6, and the like are to be believed. Could it be that the PTR decides a priori what can and cannot happen in the world and its history? And if, despite this decision, the impossible — the singular God in the singular event of Christ — happens, then it remains just that, impossible. The Macquarrie citation is the most forceful statement of the exclusivist claim to absoluteness that the PTR itself advances, despite its insistence on its own merely "hypothetical" character. This absolute claim contradicts the PTR's stated concern to foster esteem for the truths of religion. We can only hope that not all the followers of the PTR share Macquarrie's view. On the other hand, it is difficult to discover any theoretical support for this hope in the pluralist position.

This bleak prospect is borne out by the provocative question that Schmidt-Leukel calls the "crucial question" of the PTR: "ought we to wish that everyone on the planet would become Christian, or Christians of the same confession, and that all the other religions would disappear, or would this not perhaps be an unfortunate impoverishment for the religious life of humanity?" (317).

We might put the question like this: Ought we to wish that all men be saved by Christ and come to the knowledge of this truth?

Whoever, like Rahner, joins the apostles, the New Testament, and the Christian churches united with the faith of the original church in saying "Yes," should expect from the PTR what Jesus heard from his point of the pluralistic theology of religions, Schmidt-Leukel says. Should all men on earth become adherents of the PTR or followers of John Hick out of a love for world peace? Anyone who asks Schmidt-Leukel's provocative question should be ready for a tu quoque.

Jesus himself is probably the best proof that his eschatological mission does not entail the destruction of the tradition of faith in which he was brought up. In his mission to gather the eschatological people of God, Jesus began to fulfill the Jewish faith, a fulfillment constitutive of the proclamation of the kingdom. The Abba of Jesus is the God of Abraham, of Isaac, and of Jacob.

If Jesus is the incarnation of the divine Son, he is also the fulfillment, the inexhaustible enrichment, and the purification of every religion. Before the knowledge of Christ, which surpasses everything, Paul considers all that hitherto shaped his life, even his origin and religious identity, as "rubbish" (Phil. 3:8). But it is also clear that he does not throw the faith of his fathers upon the dung heap. His fight for the salvation of Israel is impressive, astounding (Rom. 9:1-5). Christ alone enables God's saving will to become concretely effective even in other religions (to the extent that they move toward him). In this sense there are many implicit mediators of salvation that convey the salvation of the one Mediator between God and man.

This does not mean that all religions are directly willed by God, much less that they are all steps in a gradual ascent to Christ. Yet this is Schmidt-Leukel's inference from the official documents of the Catholic Church concerning the relationship between Christianity and non-Christian religions

(326). He thus twists their sense to agree with his own position. God cannot found a religion that entangles him in self-contradiction. This statement presupposes, of course, the possibility of a philosophical knowledge of God, on the basis of which we can say, for example, that God cannot found a religion that attempts to manipulate him through magic. But anything in such a religion that might still, by virtue of the grace of Christ, lend itself to producing an authentic love of God offers a real chance of salvation. In other words, not every religion as such offers the possibility of salvation; it is rather whatever in that religion links its practitioner with the grace of Christ rather than drawing him away from it (*Lumen Gentium*, 16; *Nostra Aetate* [hereafter *NA*], 2). Schmidt-Leukel simply erases this nuance.

Why does God permit so many religions to exist in spite of the event of Christ? He allows them in the context of a history of salvation in which man has become alienated from him. The religions thus express man's search for God and a provisional perception and recognition of his power. This God and this power are found in Jesus. God thus leads every man to himself on a completely individual, unique path by way of the one path that he has opened up in Christ; a religious tradition can here point out the way (*NA*, 2).[24]

No One Dies for a Hypothesis — No One Can Love Hypothetically

Admittedly the PTR claims to be no more than a hypothesis. Yet one may challenge the competence of the PTR to state unequivocally that the positions it calls exclusivism and inclusivism are likewise nothing more than hypotheses (314f.). The first point is to respect the claim to truth of the other's position.

Christian theology, in any case, cannot agree to the label of "hypothetical," especially if this term is understood in the sense of a critical rationalism. Otherwise Christianity could no longer do justice to the eschatological definitiveness of its object. Jesus does not preach the hypothesis of the kingdom of God, nor does he die for a mere hypothesis.[25] In the same way,

---

24. See Bürkle, 70-73.

25. "No one dies for a hypothesis" (R. Spaemann, "Ende der Moralität?" in *Moderne oder Postmoderne?* ed. Peter Koslowski [1986], 28).

Christian faith does not understand itself as a hypothesis, for a hypothesis can always be improved through a process of verification or falsification. We can formulate real conditions in which faith can be verified or falsified: the examiner would collapse into nonbeing before he could disprove belief in eternal life. Nor would the community of researchers be consoled by the idea that the empirical examination of the hypothesis of Christian faith can occur only in the eternal vision of God.

At the center of Christianity stands a reality at once historical and personal: the eschatological presence of God in the history of Jesus as the anticipation of the fulfillment of history. Faith is rooted in this eschatological, proleptic reality. Faith is a response, in the form of a definitive *self-communication* by man, to the definitive, eschatological self-communication of God in Jesus; only by means of a personal self-entrustment to God can man correspond to God's self-revelation. Faith participates in the eschatological dynamism toward fulfillment of the kingdom of God in Jesus: the definitive quality of the act of faith is open to the full figure of its "object." Even this opening does not reduce faith to the level of a hypothesis; it makes it an act of freedom that one can perform only insofar as one has grasped the definitive enactment of his own freedom.

Man's definitive becoming through freedom can make sense — this is the conclusion of the philosophy of religion — only if death does not destroy the life that has become definitive, but rather calls forth its fulfillment in personal communion with the one, personal, free God. The fulfillment of human freedom as the making definitive of man's life presupposes the God who gives himself freely as the fulfillment of life become definitive.

Theology lives from the insight of the philosophy of religion that human freedom cannot hope to become definitive except thanks to the divine freedom that freely comes to meet it.

A "philosophical" faith or hope is therefore already a part of the human enactment of freedom.

To be sure, the outcome of the encounter between human and divine freedom cannot be deduced. Nor can it be predicted hypothetically. Freedom posits something definitive, and it answers that something with a corresponding definitiveness. Hypothetical knowledge of the object, then, cannot measure the distance between human and divine freedom; for the same reason it is unable to describe faith as the result of the encounter between these two freedoms in time.

Similarly the Christian marriage vows are not hypotheses: "Let's see if things work out." Rather they are a mutual self-communication, the pronouncement of a "Yes," and the definitive decision for this mutual self-communication. Christian marriage is definitive, even as this definitiveness opens up to ongoing appropriation and deepening. People who relate to each other only hypothetically cannot be said to love, or to have faith in, each other.

This holds analogously for man's relation to God's decision on his, man's, behalf. God wants to bind himself definitively to man in Christ. He seeks man's decision in faith, hope, and love. The saving love of God and neighbor that corresponds to God's definitive decision leaves no room for the hypothetical.

Theology, as reflection on the word of faith in love for God and neighbor, must echo this truth at the conceptual level. By way of analogy, theology initiates the practitioner into the historical revelation of the ever greater mystery of the trinitarian God, who is love and the foundation of love. True to the character of its "object," theology is consummated in doxology.

That acknowledgment of the reality of God is not hypothetical also follows if we consider that precisely this acknowledgment of the Absolute is the sine qua non for knowing the relative, hence, for making hypotheses in the first place, which, after all, are a relative form of knowledge. All finite knowledge, all scientific hypothesis, makes sense only in reference to the Absolute. The ability to grasp the Absolute (or unconditioned) as a condition of the possibility of the finite as such (of the conditioned as such) is not another instance of what the Absolute itself grounds and accounts for. The Absolute itself cannot be considered a hypothesis or a conditional reality whose truth must be demonstrated. The reality of hypothetical knowledge makes known the reality and the nonhypothetical character of the truth of the Absolute.

One might object that the possibility of making hypotheses requires only the *idea* of an Absolute. But this objection betrays a failure to understand the Absolute and, therefore, to attain the condition of the possibility of the hypothetical. Neither an infinite series of hypotheses nor a finite idea of the Absolute establishes the reality of the hypothesis. The only possible ground is the limitless reality of the Absolute itself. Absolutization of the finite spirit's knowledge and freedom is also contradictory (see above).

The scientific character of Christian theology depends upon the insight drawn from the philosophy of religion that the Absolute can be known and conceived only as such. Theology, with a philosophy of religion as its mediator, sets before us what is the ground of every hypothetical claim. It would, then, be untrue to its "object" if it considered itself to be a science of the merely hypothetical. There are, of course, theological "hypotheses," but these pertain to specific theological questions.

Theology also shows the possibility of the Absolute's self-disclosure in history. Inquiry into this historical disclosure, this event in which human freedom finds fulfillment in union with the freedom of God, is thus part and parcel of the self-actuation of freedom sustained by the hope of a (possible) divine self-gift.

One can arrive at a knowledge of the event, however, only by way of another human freedom that witnesses to having definitively taken its place within the historical definitiveness of God. Through the chain of witnesses, one's decision here and now is based on the original testimony — on the one who in his death became the definitive acceptance of God's definitiveness in history; the one who in his resurrection attains the fulfillment of his existence within the definitive eschaton.

It is, then, the category of testimony rather than hypothesis (which pertains to the nonpersonal) that reflects the nature of theology. We can show philosophically that the person represents the most intense form of being. In light of such a demonstration, it then becomes clear that personal testimony is the most intense form of the mediation of truth. The category of testimony, which is the lifeblood of Christian theology, thus receives a further proof of its universal communicability and validity.

If, then, the PTR wishes to capitalize on the self-understanding of Christian theology, it needs to abandon the plane of merely finite, limited hypothetical forms of knowledge and ascend instead to an analogical knowledge of the transcendent. Only this ascent can secure the possibility of God's eschatological definitiveness in history and of a definitive self-communication of man in faith. Only such a self-communication by man corresponds adequately to God's own definitiveness.

Linguistic Problems: The Empty Center

The clear difficulty of a dialogue between Christian theology, which owes allegiance to the church's continuous profession of faith, and the PTR is that the PTR changes the original meaning of the terms it borrows from the Christian tradition, such as "mediator of salvation." The one mediator of God's saving will is not Jesus himself, but a general predicate applicable to any number of individual cases. Examples could be multiplied.

Because of its apparent link with Christian tradition, some will undoubtedly find the PTR compatible with Christianity. Those, on the other hand, who analyze the difference of meaning of the terms used must seriously question this compatibility.

The hermeneutically reckless use of individual statements of Christian theologians like Pannenberg and Aquinas reinforces the suspicion that the PTR has yet to offer a nonreductive account not only of ecclesial Christianity but also of certain theologians and, it is to be feared, non-Christian religions as well.

One gets the impression that the biography of certain religious pluralists whom Schmidt-Leukel cites makes it even more difficult for them to convey unqualified appreciation of Christianity. Despite the "radical shift of mentality" from an evangelical exclusivism to what is in fact an exclusivist pluralism (309), there is, underlying both extremes, a common exclusive claim.

The center remains empty of meaning, because neither position attains the *universale concretum* of salvation in Christ. In place of the concrete universal is an assumption of quantitative models of the fullness of salvation. It is as if salvation were concentrated in Jesus and then spread out, in various degrees of intensity, in the other religions.

Be that as it may, it makes more sense to seek dialogue with other religions from the central strength of one's own. In this way we will respect and appreciate the self-understanding, and the strong points, of other religious traditions. The abstract starting point of the pluralists is too narrow to do justice, without reduction, to the living starting point of Christian faith.

Jesus Christ: The Absolute in History?

The Question concerning the Universal
Significance of a Historical Fact

KARL-HEINZ MENKE

A Glance at the Background History of the
Contemporary Relativizing of Christian Claims

The first document issued by those known as the theologians of religious pluralism exploded on the scene like a bomb. In 1977, after a three-year discussion, seven Christian theologians of various confessions published a small collection of essays entitled *The Myth of God Incarnate*, and thereby provoked an enormous backlash.[1]

The most obvious target of this polemic was the incarnation Christol-

---

1. *The Myth of God Incarnate*, ed. John Hick (London, 1977). Citations are from the German edition, *Wurde Gott Mensch? Der Mythos vom fleischgewordenen Gott* (Gütersloh, 1979). Only a few weeks after this collection of essays came out, a collection of critical responses appeared in a volume edited by Michael Green: *The Truth of God Incarnate* (London, 1977). Some of the more significant contributions to the debate are N. Anderson, *The Mystery of the Incarnation* (London, 1978); D. Cupitt, *The Debate about Christ* (London, 1979); M. Goulder, ed., *Incarnation and Myth: The Debate Continued* (London, 1983); A. E. Harvey, ed., *God Incarnate: Story and Belief* (London, 1981); R. T. Herbert, *Paradox and Identity in Theology* (Ithaca, N.Y., 1979); J. Hick, *God Has Many Names* (London, 1980); J. P. Mackey, *Jesus, the Man and the Myth: A Contemporary Christology* (London, 1982); T. F. Torrance, ed., *The Incarnation: Ecumenical Studies in the Nicene-Constantinopolitan Creed, A.D. 381* (Edinburgh, 1981); K. Ward, *Holding Fast to God: A Reply to Don Cupitt* (London, 1983); M. Wiles, *Faith and the Mystery of God* (London, 1982); J. Hick, *The Metaphor of God Incarnate* (Westminster, 1994).

ogy of the Oxford movement.[2] As the editor John Hick underscores in the collection's introduction, beginning in the middle of the nineteenth-century this movement had consistently centered Anglican spirituality and theology on the mystery of the incarnation. Doing so, they encouraged the supplanting of rational scrutiny by fideistic belief in the letter of Scripture. The Oxford movement thought in terms of a Christology from above, but not genuinely from a trinitarian perspective. The difference between the Logos and the Pneuma received as little reflection as the relationship between Christology and ecclesiology. In light of this inadequacy a collection of essays published in 1889 under the title *Lux Mundi* is significant.[3] The well-known conservative authors — with Charles Gore (1853-1932) foremost among them[4] — felt themselves challenged, through dialogue with historical-critical exegesis and the theory of evolution, to correct certain one-sided tendencies. On the one hand they sought to do justice to the Jesus of the synoptics by a doctrine of the self-emptying of divine attributes *(kenosis)*[5] and a doctrine of the reciprocal "enhypostasis" of Christ's divine and human consciousnesses.[6] On the other hand they stretched the event

2. It is possible to distinguish four periods in the development of the Oxford movement: (a) the "Tractarian" period (1833-41), during which the leading figures of the movement presented their ideas in popular pamphlets; (b) the "ritualism" period, lasting until 1870, during which many Catholic rites were introduced into the Church of England; (c) the period from 1870 to 1960, during which Anglo-Catholicism increasingly become the dominant force in the Church of England; and (d) the period after Vatican II, during which there emerged a nearly insurmountable chasm between the conservative Anglicans of the Oxford movement and the liberal Anglicans that gathered around Bishop John A. T. Robinson (the author of *Honest to God*).

3. The collection entitled *Lux Mundi* is just the most important volume of a whole series: for example, *Essays and Reviews* (1860); *Foundations* (1912); *Essays Catholic and Critical* (1962); and *Soundings* (1962). The eleven authors of *Lux Mundi* (1889) had without exception some link to Oxford University. In relation to the Greek Fathers and the idealistic philosophy of T. H. Greens (1836-82), they were concerned above all with reconciling an incarnation Christology with historical-critical exegesis and the theory of evolution.

4. In addition to C. Gore, this group included E. S. Talbot, H. Scott Holland, J. R. Illingworth, and R. C. Moberly.

5. In a nutshell, this kenotic Christology affirms that, according to Phil. 2:6ff., the preexistent Son renounced all divine characteristics so completely that, in the event of the incarnation, he preserved the integrity of his identity only in relation to his personhood (i.e., his relationship to his Father). Cf. in this respect, M. Breidert, *Die kenotische Christologie des 19. Jahrhunderts* (Gütersloh, 1977).

6. From Frank Weston (*The One Christ: An Enquiry into the Manner of the Incarnation* [London, 1907]) to Thomas V. Morris (*The Logic of God Incarnate* [Ithaca, N.Y., and London,

of the incarnation so broadly throughout the whole of creation and salvation history that it would make more sense to speak of God's progressive self-revelation through the Spirit than of the unique event of the Son's incarnation. In her *Habilitationsschrift*, provocatively entitled "Incarnation or Inspiration?" Ulrike Link-Wieczorek characterized this approach as the pneumatological assimilation of the doctrine of the incarnation,[7] and described in this respect a steady development from John R. Illingworth to Geoffrey W. Lampe.[8]

Less radical than Lampe's Spirit Christology is the book published just a few years ago by the Dutchman Piet Schoonenberg. But this book nevertheless makes reference to Lampe. Speaking critically, Schoonenberg remarks that Lampe's "denial of an Incarnation in the strict sense is based not only on the denial of the pre-existence of any second (or third) Person in God . . . , but also and primarily on the denial of the Personhood of the glorified Christ."[9] In opposition to Lampe, Schoonenberg pleads for a trinitarian foundation for Spirit Christology. Nevertheless, in everything else he distinguishes himself only marginally from the English theologian. He presents a salvation-historical conception of the Trinity, in which God allows his own identity to be so thoroughly determined by the relationship to creation, and in particular to the creature Jesus, that the end result is a "personalizing" of God's "external forms" (Logos and Pneuma). Schoonenberg speaks of an "eschatologically open Trinity," which becomes actual-

1986]), we can trace the notion that Jesus' divine consciousness had at every moment complete access to his human consciousness, even while, by contrast, his human consciousness only had a very limited access to his divine consciousness.

7. Cf. U. Link-Wieczorek, *Inkarnation oder Inspiration? Christologische Grundfragen in der Diskussion mit britischer anglikanischer Theologie*, Forschungen zur systematischen und ökumenischen Theologie 84 (Göttingen, 1998), esp. 236-97.

8. In his contribution to *Lux Mundi*, John R. Illingworth treated the problem of the reconcilability of incarnation Christology and an evolutionary worldview. His response tended in the direction of a gradualistic Christology, in which the difference between the Son and the Spirit grew less and less distinct: between the immanence of the Logos, identified with the divine Spirit, in Christ and his presence in all other creatures, there is only a difference of degree. In Geoffrey W. Lampe's "Spirit-Christology" (*God as Spirit: The Bampton Lectures, 1976* [Oxford, 1977]), there is a denial of any trinitarian foundation for Christology. Lampe relativizes the hypostasis of the Son by calling it a projection of the historical Jesus and his relationship to the Father into the essence of God.

9. P. Schoonenberg, *Der Geist, das Wort und der Sohn: Eine Geist-Christologie*, trans. W. Immler (Regensburg, 1992), 58.

ized through the incarnation of the Logos and Pneuma, a process he refers to as "personalization." But this horizon leaves no room for understanding the title "Mother of God" that Ephesus ascribed to Mary, nor for the fact that Jesus is already born as the "Son of God." Thus Schoonenberg does not see the Logos and the Pneuma as hypostases, but rather as biblical metaphors characterizing the two different ways in which God makes himself present.[10]

In relation to the Oxford movement's transformation of an incarnation Christology into a Trinity-denying theology that levels the difference between the Logos and the Pneuma, the *Myth of God Incarnate* authors' ideas were less a revolution than a result. The book was experienced as a revolution only by those who had failed to see that the drift of the Oxford incarnation Christology toward a "Spirit Christology" could not avoid giving rise in its wake to a gradualism and a functionalism. Perry Schmidt-Leukel, who more than anyone else carried John Hick's Christology into the arena of German academic theology, offers the following typology in his first study in fundamental theology:

> *Gradualistic Christology:* According to this understanding, the affirmation of the Incarnation implies that there is no essential difference between Jesus and all other human beings, but only a difference of degree. All human beings are in a certain sense connected with the reality of the *Logos,* the divine Spirit, the immanent presence of God, and so on, even if they involve themselves with this reality to a vastly different extent in each case. Jesus allowed his life to be entirely determined by God. . . .
> *Functionalistic Christology:* According to this approach, the affirmation of the Incarnation refers primarily to the effect Jesus had, to his significance for the religious history of humanity. Jesus is the one who reveals, insofar as his life sets in motion a process of new knowledge of God and a new human relationship to God. God is present in this process, which has Jesus as its source. It is not so important how Jesus himself lived precisely, whether he was truly without any sin whatsoever, and so forth;

---

10. Given the assumption that God becomes personalized as Son and Spirit only through his relation to creation, or to man, the pneumatological corrections Schoonenberg makes to his earlier publications are of little import. While in previous publications he demanded a reversal of the scholastic doctrine of enhypostasis (not the "enhypostasis" of the human nature in the person of the Logos, but the reverse!), he now speaks of a "reciprocal enhypostasis" (Schoonenberg, 153).

what is important is the impression that he left behind and which the Holy Scriptures bear witness to in the Christ-images and the words of Jesus.[11]

John Hick, whom Schmidt-Leukel ranks among the greatest theologians, sets forth a Christology that is at once gradualistic and functionalistic in *The Myth of God Incarnate*. His thinking remains enmeshed within the same Trinity-denying identification of the Logos and the Pneuma that we find in the authors of *Lux Mundi*. He merely brings the ideas of the Oxfordian Spirit Christology to a sharper point insofar as he attempts to dialogue with analytical philosophy and accommodates the self-understanding of non-Christian religions.

Hick accounts for the progression in Christology from the statement "Jesus is the Son of God" to "Jesus is God the Son" as a process of projecting the historical Jesus' relation to the Father into the essence of God himself. Hick clearly borrows this idea from Lampe. Moreover, for Hick the affirmation "Jesus is God the Son" is a misguided attempt "to interpret a metaphor, which functioned as religious myth, in a metaphysical sense, and thus no longer to understand it as a metaphorical statement about a figure existing in our historical-empirical reality but as a descriptive statement concerning an essence with trans-historical reality."[12] Hick distinguishes "mythological truth" from "literal truth." Myths, he claims, are an attempt "to bring a certain set of values to expression and to foster a certain behavior."[13] A myth for him is "a story that is told, but which is not literally true, or an idea or an image ascribed to a person or thing, but which does not apply in a literal sense. Instead, it is meant to produce a certain behavior or representation in its hearers."[14] Hick plays the pragmatic function of the myth off of its semantic function. He views the statement "Jesus is God the Son" as a metaphor, which expresses Jesus' significance for us in total indifference to its actual truth content. Thus Hick views the struggles of the early councils to grasp the uniqueness of Christ as necessarily vain attempts to translate metaphors into descriptive statements, myth into metaphysics.

11. P. Schmidt-Leukel, *Grundkurs Fundamentaltheologie: Eine Einführung in die Grundlagen des christlichen Glaubens* (Munich, 1999), 218f.

12. I. U. Dalferth, *Der auferweckte Gekreuzigte: Zur Grammatik der Christologie* (Tübingen, 1994), 12f.

13. Hick, *Wurde Gott Mensch?* 187 n. 1.

14. Hick, *Wurde Gott Mensch?* 188.

Schmidt-Leukel adopts a nearly identical position.[15] In an essay published in the *Münchner theologische Zeitschrift* in 1998, he describes at length the unbridgeable chasm lying between God and any creaturely medium of revelation;[16] at the same time, however, he stresses that "God reveals *himself,* he allows himself to be experienced by human beings and encounters them in history — indeed, in the *whole* of history, and not just in a tiny fragment of it."[17]

Schmidt-Leukel explains that we can unite these two poles — "persisting transcendence" and "God's real self-revelation in history" — by means of the very same categories that run through the "Spirit Christology" of the Anglican *Lux Mundi* authors like a red thread. He draws no distinction between Logos and Pneuma. Indeed, for Schmidt-Leukel, just as for Hick or Lampe, the whole of creation and the whole of history is a continual process of the self-revelation of God, i.e., of the divine Logos or Holy Spirit. In his words,

> Only in relation to the oneness of God, a oneness that lies beyond all counting and numbers, can we speak meaningfully of a single mediator of salvation, which is no one else but God himself in his self-revelation. This one *Logos,* which according to traditional belief fills the cosmos, is the sole mediator, the one who makes love of God and love of neighbor possible. Only in this sense are we able to say, for example, that Abraham is already a sharer in salvation through the mediation of Christ, and that it is in fact the *Logos* Christ who says in John's Gospel: "Even before Abraham was, I am" (Jn 8:58). This *Logos* took shape in the life of Jesus in a unique way, but nevertheless he pervades the whole of creation. And thus

---

15. Cf. P. Schmidt-Leukel, *Theologie der Religionen: Probleme, Optionen, Argumente,* Beiträge zur Fundamentaltheologie und Religionsphilosophie 1 (Frankfurt, 1997), esp. 502-82.

16. "We can and we must speak of God using the images, names, and concepts that we have borrowed from finite reality. Nevertheless, we must at the same time keep in mind that we are dealing with a reality that transcends everything finite, and thus one that cannot properly be grasped through any mode of speech, except negative speech. We must therefore clearly distinguish, on the one hand, between the divine reality in its infinite, inconceivable and ineffable Spirit, and, on the other, the divine reality such as it is brought to expression through the images and concepts derived from the human field of experience." P. Schmidt-Leukel, "Was will die pluralistische Religionstheologie?" *Münchner theologische Zeitschrift* 49 (1998): 307-34, 259.

17. Schmidt-Leukel, "Was will die pluralistische Religionstheologie?" 331.

the one *Logos*, who was incarnate in Jesus, makes possible a multiplicity of different, historical and concrete mediations of salvation.[18]

In the passage quoted, the name "Christ" is a synonym for the omnipresence of the divine Logos, or the divine Pneuma, in each and every creature, and in every meaningful moment in history. "Christ" is therefore nothing more than the Logos of Stoic philosophy. In this context Schmidt-Leukel cites the Anglican John Macquarrie's statement "that the Incarnation does not represent any singularity or unique occurrence in world history, but is instead a constant characteristic of God's relationship to his creation."[19] And he is particularly wont to refer to Karl Rahner, since this latter characterizes the event of the incarnation as "the single highest case of the realization of the essence *(Wesensvollzug)* of the human reality."[20] But Schmidt-Leukel takes Rahner's point a step further:

> The notion that there is a supreme realization of the human essence presupposes that there are various other instances of its realization, which are lower and less successful, but nevertheless instances of the same essence. Couldn't there then be in principle other realizations of this essence that are just as high and just as successful? Indeed, if what is at issue is truly the realization of the human *essence,* aren't we compelled to take this possibility seriously? Wouldn't it be exceedingly surprising if, among all human beings, only a single one ever came to a full realization of the human essence? Wouldn't this be all the more surprising if we take for granted that God urges all human beings to precisely this level of realization, that God's grace-filled self-gift to human beings is thus always and everywhere already striving to take concrete shape in the existence of each human being?[21]

This commentary twists Rahner's statement into saying precisely the opposite of what he intended.[22] For when Rahner speaks of a "single

18. Schmidt-Leukel, "Was will die pluralistische Religionstheologie?" 327.

19. Schmidt-Leukel, "Was will die pluralistische Religionstheologie?" 325. Cf. J. Macquarrie, *The Mediators* (London, 1995), 149.

20. K. Rahner, *Grundkurs des Glaubens: Einführung in den Begriff des Christentums* (Freiburg, 1977), 216.

21. Schmidt-Leukel, "Was will die pluralistische Religionstheologie?" 324 n. 16.

22. On this point see Schmidt-Leukel, "Was will die pluralistische Religionstheologie?" 532-42 n. 15.

highest realization of the essence," he wants to make clear, on the one hand, that God cannot express himself in just any creature, but once and for all in a single human being. At the same time, avoiding the problematic concepts "nature" and "person," he wants to insist that the uniqueness of this single human being, in whom God has de facto expressed himself, is an integral component of the uniqueness of the relationship to the Father by virtue of which Jesus Christ is identical with the person of the eternal Logos within the conditions of space and time. A glance at the seventh step in his basic course suffices to reveal the one-sidedness of Schmidt-Leukel's interpretation. Rahner himself, indeed, argues simultaneously from below and from above. We are able to speak of the incarnation as the highest instance of the realization of the essence of the human reality, he explains, because man is the sole creature who can transcend himself because he is endowed with spirit. However, if we take God as our starting point — i.e., if we proceed christologically from above — it follows that when God becomes man, he does not only use a human being as an instrument of expression but in fact expresses himself as man.[23] A human being, though, is always a unique reality. If the individuality of a human being is supposed to form part of his self-expression, God cannot be separated from the uniqueness of the human being in whom he communicates himself. This is why Rahner explicitly calls the event of the incar-

---

23. As long as "the finite mediation of the divine self-expression does not in the strict and proper sense present the very reality of God himself, it will always remain provisional and able to be improved upon, because it is finite, and in its finitude is simply not the reality of God himself. God can therefore always surpass it by a new positing of the finite. It follows that if Jesus, in whom God's self-communication is 'present' for us and the whole of humanity in an absolute way as promise and affirmation, is truly the definitive and unsurpassable promise and affirmation, then we have to say that Jesus is not only posited by God but is God himself. But if this promise, which is itself a human reality, is graced as absolute, and if this promise is truly and absolutely of God himself, then it is the absolute belongingness of a human reality to God; in other words, properly understood, it is precisely what we call the *unio hypostatica.*" Rahner, 202 n. 20. Because the real promise God makes to us of himself is the human reality, or the fact, of Jesus of Nazareth, "then the unity between the one who promises and the promise itself need not be understood merely 'morally,' as for example the unity between a human word (a mere sign) and God, but must be understood as an irrevocable unity between this human reality and God, as a unity that eliminates the possibility of a separation between the revealer and the revealed, and thus makes that which is truly humanly revealed and promised to us into a reality of God himself. And this is precisely what the *unio hypastatica* means, this and nothing else" (202 n. 20).

nation of the eternal Logos in the one man Jesus Christ "unique" and "unrepeatable."[24]

No Christology without Trinitarian Theology: The Condition
of Possibility of the Presence of the Absolute in History

Perry Schmidt-Leukel believes there is an anachronistic desire bound up with the exclusivistic understanding of the incarnation, namely, a desire that everyone on earth should become Christian.[25] Not a few representatives of the pluralistic theology of religions

> posit a causal connection between the early Church's confession of the uniqueness of Jesus Christ as mediator of salvation and the crimes committed in Europe and in the world at the time of Christianity's dominance in society. A literalistic understanding of the pre-existence and incarnation of Jesus Christ, and of his divine Sonship, is responsible for the spread of Christian anti-Semitism, and also the violent proceedings against heretics. A triumphalistic understanding of the Church, such as the one expressed in the sentence *extra ecclesiam nulla salus*, contributed to the violence of the missions and to European colonialism, in the wake of which self-sufficient cultures and religions were driven out and destroyed. Finally, the causes of the religious wars in Christian Europe can be traced back to a dogmatic understanding of propositional truths concerning salvation. Only a decisive renunciation of any dogmatically interpreted Christianity, whether it be exclusivistic or inclusivistic, will allow us to acknowledge God's revelation in all religions and to respect these religions as equally justified

24. Michael Schulz ("Anfragen an die Pluralistische Religionstheologie: *Einer* ist Gott, *nur Einer* auch Mittler," *Münchner theologische Zeitschrift* 51 [2000]: 125-50) stresses that, unlike Schmidt-Leukel, Rahner relates the whole of humanity as collectively guilty to the one mediator who takes away the sin of the whole world (cf. 143f.). And if Rahner fails to serve as chief witness in support of the pluralistic theology of religions, for that matter so does Aquinas. "For *Thomas*, the hypostatic union of the divine and human natures in the one and only subject of existence, i.e., the Person of the *Logos*, represents the highest unity conceivable outside of God's own unity. That is why the Incarnation occurs only in this supreme form of divine-human unity" (143).
25. Cf. Schmidt-Leukel, "Was will die pluralistische Religionstheologie?" 317 n. 317.

manifestations of the divine in the religious experience of each and every human being.[26]

These assertions result from an inability to make distinctions. For the absolute affirmation of a finite reality is something altogether different from the Absolute's own making himself present in the medium of the finite. The questionable affirmation that the creature Jesus (the true humanity of Jesus) is identical with God (with the Absolute) is something utterly distinct from what the tradition calls the "hypostatic union."

Of course, one may wish to insist that a theologian who grounds his Christology in trinitarian theology is in no position to do justice to biblical Christology.[27] But this altogether debatable view is something quite differ-

---

26. G. L. Müller, "Erkenntnistheoretische Grundprobleme einer Theologie der Religionen," *Forum Katholische Theologie* 15 (1999): 161-79, 168.

27. According to Pannenberg, the traditional incarnation Christology is based on a fiction, "as though God were already God in the fullest sense outside of Jesus Christ and without this historical human being, as though it were a secondary matter that he decided to become incarnate in this human being: as though it were precisely this God, understood as existing prior to the incarnation, and then understood as deciding upon the incarnation; but if this is the case, how can God be understood as revealing himself in the man Jesus in such a way that the things that properly characterize him as a human being do not obscure God's divinity but precisely bring it to expression? How could God thus be understood as united with the person of Jesus if he possessed his divinity already independently of the event of his revelation in such a way that this event would have no further significance for that divinity? How is it possible for an event occurring outside of God's essence to reveal that essence? On the other hand, how can we bring this understanding into unity with the fundamental trinitarian knowledge that the man Jesus Christ belongs as Person to the eternal essence of God himself? . . . This Greek *chorismos* in the notion of the eternal and inaccessible God as subject of the event of the Incarnation, this fundamental Christological separation between this God's divinity and the historical man Jesus of Nazareth, casts a peculiar light on the well-known fact that Christologies constructed on notions of the Incarnation have never yet been able to account for the concrete, historical man Jesus of Nazareth: Could the reason perhaps be that such Christologies from the outset are missing the properly Christian notion of God as essentially one with the Person of this man? . . . The decisive defect in 'Christologies from above' consists in the fact that they fail on precisely what ought to be their strongpoint in the face of all the reflection that is fixed on the finitude of the merely historical: They fail to conceive the historical figure of Jesus of Nazareth from the perspective of God's divinity itself as his revelation. Indeed, theologies that start from the historical figure of Jesus and its significance also fail on this point insofar as the idea of God remains external to their thinking rather than functioning as an interpretive instrument that invites an examination of the person and history of Jesus" (W. Pannenberg, "Christologie und

ent from Piet Schoonenberg's, Hans Küng's, Karl-Josef Kuschel's, Perry Schmidt-Leukel's, or Karl-Heinz Ohlig's[28] express denial of any affirmation of an immanent Trinity.

If Jesus Christ is the savior of all people of all times; if Paul speaks of his faith *in* Jesus as the Christ (Gal. 1:16); if Jesus in John 14:9 says "He who sees me sees the Father"; if John characterizes Jesus as the way, the truth, and the life (John 14:6); and if the eating and drinking of his flesh and blood (cf. John 6:51-65) means communion with the Father, then one cannot claim that the trinitarian and christological terminology of the early councils represents a falsification of biblical data.

According to Karl-Josef Kuschel,[29] it would be no great loss if the classical doctrine of the Trinity and the doctrine of the hypostatic union and the two natures in Christ were to die out as a time-bound formulation of faith, just as the "old metaphysics" has similarly faded away, because our age's nonmetaphysical understanding of reality has allowed us once again to enter fully into the biblical proclamation and its horizon of reality, and this reality should not be interpreted metaphysically or ontologically. Kuschel does not consider that even in this case speech about God raises the suspicion of being deduced from reality by means of concepts, since it occurs in the narrative and historical categories of the Bible. Of course, a metaphysics expressed in the categories of experience and personal encounter is distinct from one expressed through rational analyses. But is the claim to meaning any less metaphysical if it clothes itself in the categories of personal experience rather than in concepts and arguments?

Theologie," in Pannenberg, *Grundfragen Systematischer Theologie: Gesammelte Aufsätze*, vol. 2 [Göttingen, 1980], 129-45, 133f.).

In June 1999 Georg Essen, in his as yet unpublished *Habilitationsschrift* for the Catholic theology faculty at Münster ("Die Freiheit Jesu: Der neuchalkedonische Enhypostasiebegriff im Horizont neuzeitlicher Subjekt- und Personphilosophie"), developed an extremely interesting alternative to Pannenberg's attempt to understand the divinity of Jesus on the basis of his relationship to the Father. Drawing on Hermann Krings's analyses of freedom, he develops the notion that Jesus lives the personhood he receives from the absolute love of the Father, i.e., he lives the freedom of the inner-trinitarian Son, as true man in the chasm between formal unconditionality and material limitation.

28. Cf. K.-H. Ohlig, *Ein Gott in drei Personen? Vom Vater Jesu zum 'Mysterium' der Trinität* (Mainz, 1999).

29. Cf. K. J. Kuschel, *Geboren vor aller Zeit? Der Streit um Christi Ursprung* (Munich, 1990), esp. 628-91.

Even disregarding the fact that we cannot recover a naive contemporaneity with the consciousness of the biblical authors, we can no more isolate the biblical mind-set from the event to which it bears witness (i.e., the historical self-revelation of the Absolute) than we could any other mind-set. The privilege of the biblical mind-set lies in the fact that it serves as a measure for every subsequent mind-set. But any theology that in a "biblistic" manner attempts to bracket out the two-thousand-year history of the transmission of the event of Christ condemns itself to the museums.

Of course, it is a question of interpretation if one characterizes the history of Jesus of Nazareth in the strict sense as God's self-revelation. But the early councils unreservedly take for granted that Jesus Christ is not a prophet or a metaphor, but God's own self-expression. From that time forward at least, no one who calls himself a Christian can speak of Christ without speaking at the same time of the Absolute (i.e., of God). Or, in other words, the question whether Christology is rooted in the Trinity is in no way a question of biblical or Hellenistic modes of thinking. Only if we presuppose a trinitarian understanding of God, only if God himself is Word (Logos), that is, Relation, and only if God is Spirit, i.e., unity within difference, can he relate himself to something outside of himself and therefore to creation in such a way that it may belong to him without losing its integrity as being created.[30]

In my opinion it would not be honest if, in relation to the Jews for example, we were to hide the fact that Christianity's self-understanding stands or falls with this affirmation. As the systematic theologian from Münster, Thomas Pröpper, formulates it in his commentary on Tiemo Rainer Peters's notion of a Christology after Auschwitz, "This affirmation, and thus the perception of Jesus' history as the definitive proof of the decisive Love of the God of Israel for man (and more precisely the presence and the self-gift of God in the unconditionality of his love, made present and real in Jesus), implies indeed in the strictest sense the affirmation of the *self-revelation* of God and . . . consequently that, from this point forward, . . . there can be no more explanation or clarification

---

30. Gerhard Ludwig Müller (cf. n. 26 above, 169-74) distinguishes three axioms in the pluralistic theology of religions which he takes to be symptomatic of an absence of a doctrine of the Trinity: (1) the axiom of the fundamental impossibility of communication between God and man in word and deed; (2) the axiom of God's incapacity for incarnation; and (3) the axiom of the inability of human nature to be taken up into a divine hypostasis.

of the being and essence of God except as determined through Jesus Christ."[31]

This position would become anti-Semitic only if we failed to acknowledge a distinction between Christianity and Judaism, and, for example, characterized both the Torah and Jesus Christ in the same way (without distinguishing further) as the "Word of God." In this case we would be subordinating the Jews to the Christians, saying that Jews characterize the Torah as the Word of God just as Christians do Jesus Christ. But such a subordination, in fact, would not be true to the facts. If one assumes a mono-subjectivistic understanding of God, it is impossible to claim that God can bind himself to a creature without either thereby obliterating the creature with his divinity or ceasing himself to be God. Judaism is essentially determined by the question: How can human words be the Word of God without compromising the transcendence of Yahweh, a transcendence heightened by the biblical prohibition of images and the uttering of the name of God?

When Erich Zenger claims that Israel's Scriptures are "in and of themselves the Word of God; they are neither provisional nor preparatory, but the definitive Word,"[32] he unwittingly denies the distance the Jews affirm between God himself and his Torah. To point out a difference between Christianity and Judaism does not mean that Christianity surpasses Judaism; what is harmful to the other is hushing up and hiding the things that make a difference, because it represents a failure to take the other seriously. Since there cannot be any such thing as a surpassable Word of God, Jesus Christ is not the surpassing of the Torah. Rather, as Irenaeus puts it, he is "the One Word in the many words" (*Adversus haereses* 2.28.3).

What Allows Us to Recognize the Absolute in History?

What Karl Rahner, Hans Urs von Balthasar, Wolfhart Pannenberg, or Jürgen Moltmann all mean to affirm in their description of the relationship between the immanent and economic Trinity is that the history of Jesus is inseparable from what we call the eternal God. Needless to say, af-

31. T. Pröpper, "Wegmarken zu einer Christologie nach Auschwitz," in *Christologie nach Auschwitz: Stellungnahmen im Anschluss an Thesen von Tiemo Rainer Peters,* ed. J. Manemann and J. B. Metz (Münster, 1998), 135-46, 143.

32. E. Zenger, *Das erste Testament: Die jüdische Bibel und die Christen* (Düsseldorf, 1991), 138.

firming the inseparability of the immanent from the economic Trinity asserts a fact but does not explain what makes knowledge of the Absolute in history possible.

The question how Jesus could be recognized as the Christ cannot in my opinion be answered by saying that God bore witness that the crucified one was risen by granting visions to those who witnessed the resurrection or by sending the Holy Spirit. Regardless of whose side one takes in the debate between Hans Kessler and Hansjürgen Verweyen over the interpretation of the paschal event,[33] one still has to face the problem of the eschatological mediation of the Absolute through the particular man Jesus in the space of his earthly life.

It seems to me that recent theology has above all two responses to offer to this question. The first lies in Balthasar's gestalt aesthetics; the second can be found in the Freiburger fundamental theologian Hansjürgen Verweyen's attempt to work out a philosophically rigorous concept of the incarnation through a phenomenology of the imaging of the Unconditional in the conditional.

"Gestalt" as the Phenomenon of a Direct Proportionality between the "Concretum" and the "Universale": Jesus Christ as the "Universale Concretissimum"

Balthasar describes the gnostic identification of the finite with the nothing as the "way of appearance." What he has in mind here is, for example, the play patterns of the Asiatic traditions, but also the various faces of the "Faustian

33. Verweyen challenged Kessler to a debate, which took place through the following essays: H. Kessler, *Sucht den Lebenden nicht bei den Toten: Die Auferstehung Jesu Christi in biblischer, fundamentaltheologischer und systematischer Sicht* (Düsseldorf, 1985); H. Verweyen, "Rezension zu H. Kessler *(op. cit.)*," *Zeitschrift für katholische Theologie* 108 (1986): 71-74; H. Kessler, "Irdischer Jesus, Kreuzestod und Osterglaube: Zu Rezensionen von A. Schmied und H. Verweyen," *Theologie und Glaube* 32 (1989): 219-29; H. Verweyen, *Gottes letztes Wort: Grundriß der Fundamentaltheologie* (Düsseldorf, 1991), 441-65; Verweyen, "'Auferstehung': ein Wort verstellt die Sache," in *Osterglaube ohne Auferstehung? Diskussion mit Gerd Lüdemann*, ed. H. Verweyen (Freiburg, 1995) (= QD 155), 105-44; H. Kessler, "Erörterung der neuesten Kontroversen und aktuellen Fragen," in Kessler, *Sucht den Lebenden nicht bei den Toten: Die Auferstehung Jesu Christi, Neuausgabe mit ausführlicher Erörterung der aktuellen Fragen* (Würzburg, 1995), 419-63; H. Verweyen, *Botschaft eines Toten? Den Glauben rational verantworten* (Regensburg, 1997).

Man," who denies his finitude by seeking to leap beyond his limitations.[34] For him Christianity is the only worldview that understands the finite not as imperfection but as the ever unique locus of Being in its fullness *(actus essendi)*.

In accord with Thomas Aquinas,[35] Balthasar characterizes the *actus essendi* as that which at one and the same time binds all beings together and distinguishes them from one another. "Being," i.e., the *actus essendi*, is thus neither a univocal nor an equivocal term, insofar as a concept abstracts either the universal or the individual from reality. Being is not a concept, but perhaps something more like a relationship. The more a particular being expresses a relation to the other, the more beautiful it is, the higher it stands in the hierarchy of the real. Balthasar speaks of the gestalt of a particular creature in terms of radiant beauty. By the concept "gestalt" he means "a totality of parts and elements, which is grasped as such and which subsists in itself; in order to be itself, however, it has need not only of an 'environment' (a 'surrounding world': *Um-welt*), but finally of Being as a whole, and in this need, it becomes, as Cusanus says, a 'compact' representation of the 'Absolute.'"[36] Balthasar describes an ascending

---

34. Because each person who possesses the self-consciousnesses of his own "I" always already has an awareness of Being as a whole, and because he realizes that this awareness refers him beyond all contingent beings to an absolute Being, he can be himself only *in* affirming this movement beyond. The moment he asserts either himself or another person or thing as absolute, he flees from his dependence, finitude, and temporality in the Faustian vision of an "overman" (Nietzsche), a classless society (Marx), or a timeless nirvana (Buddhism), and thus collapses the tension between Being and being.

35. Though he makes no reference to Balthasar, Klaus Obenauer has worked out an interpretation of the event of the incarnation on the basis of the Thomistic understanding of Being, which shows an unmistakable affinity with Balthasar's own reflections. Cf. K. Obenauer, *Thomistische Metaphysik und Trinitätstheologie: Sein — Geist — Gott — Dreifaltigkeit — Gnade* (Münster, 2000), esp. 113-22.

36. Balthasar, *Herrlichkeit*, vol. III/1/1, *Im Raum der Metaphysik*, 2nd ed. (Einsiedeln, 1975), 30. In another place Balthasar defines gestalt as "never a mere unity, which in a second moment differentiates itself, or a mere fragmented multiplicity . . . , which for one reason or another 'arranges' itself into a unity. In every case, unity and multiplicity are equiprimordial, while it is nevertheless always the power of the unity to unfold its own fulness in the multiplicity of the gestalt and of the particularity of the organs of apprehension. Presumably, something analogous can be said of the trinitarian mystery: God is the one who reveals the fulness of Being in the trinitarian 'gestalt' of divinity; even though God's divinity cannot be posited prior to or above the Father, which would be Arianism, it is the Father who, in order to reveal his own fulness, begets the Son and, with him, generates the Spirit" (Balthasar, *Theodramatik*, vol. III, *Die Handlung* [Einsiedeln, 1980], 382).

array of creaturely gestalts, which reach their peak in the human being, who, because he is endowed with spirit, is the sole creature who can relate himself to all beings.[37] At the same time, however, he is also the only one who can distort his gestalt by withdrawing into himself. Because the human being becomes "concrete" to the extent that he realizes his relationship to the other not only in the abstraction of his thinking but also in the self-transcendence of his "being-for," i.e., love, he stands among all creatures as the most perfect manifestation of the direct proportionality between universal generality and singular particularity that characterizes all of reality.

Three aspects of Balthasar's Christology come to light against this background:

1. The *"concretum"* of an individual human being poses no obstacle to the self-expressive capacity of the Being that comprehends all beings (i.e., of the *"universale"*), but, precisely to the contrary, the more a human being is "himself," that is, the more "concrete" he becomes, the more he reveals the universal, i.e., the meaning of all being.

2. If the meaning of all being — i.e., God — wishes to communicate himself in creation and history, this can happen only in the creature that can relate itself to all being. Thus he can communicate himself only in human being, or more precisely, only in an *individual* human being, because there is no real relationship (i.e., self-transcendence or love) to the other except that of an *individual* human being.

3. Whenever a human being becomes "himself," i.e., becomes "concrete," to such an extent that he does perfect justice to the otherness of *every* other through his self-transcendence or love, we may call that human being the *"universale concretissimum"* or the "figure of glory" *(Herrlichkeitsgestalt)*.

The man Jesus, in Balthasar's thought, is thus "the figure of glory," insofar as he reaches, with his self-transcendence (love), which is identical with the divinity of the Son, into the hell of the sinners who seal themselves up in isolation. The "figure of glory," Jesus Christ, "comprehends"

37. On this point see J. Disse, *Metaphysik der Singularität: Eine Hinführung am Leitfaden der Philosophie Hans Urs von Balthasars,* Philosophische Theologie 7 (Vienna, 1996), esp. 213-21.

(unterfasst) the most extreme otherness imaginable, i.e., hell itself. That is why he is the *"universale concretissimum."*

What Balthasar means by the verb "comprehend" *(unterfassen)* ought not be identified with Hegel's notion of "overtaking" *(einholen)*, despite the affinity between these two thinkers. In Hegel's philosophy of religion God is "Spirit" insofar as he is no longer a monolithic "I," but is rather the Father who is in the Son and the Son who is in the Father, without allowing this unity to eliminate *(aufheben)* the difference of the Father from the Son and the Son from the Father. God is *Absolute* Spirit for Hegel because he seeks to be himself in the other. This is why, in the Son, he enters into creation, which cannot be a mere instrument or object of God because of his personality (freedom); it is, further, why he enters into man, and indeed into a wholly unique man, so that we can say of this man that he is "the" Son; and he enters into this individual all the way into the tiny corner in which finitude cowers, all the way to the extremity of sin and death; and he overtakes even these extreme points of otherness into his Son. That is why each person, who acquires the consciousness of unity with the Father by "putting on" the consciousness of the Son in faith, is included in the movement of the Absolute Spirit that overtakes all things; and why every believer, who comes to himself in the other through love without eliminating his otherness, participates in the reconciliation of all beings in the Holy Spirit, which is the spirit of the community.

This brief glance at Hegel's philosophy of religion suffices to make clear wherein the roots of all "Spirit Christologies" of the nineteenth and twentieth centuries lie, insofar as these Christologies would rather speak of the history of God (i.e., of the Absolute Spirit's historical coming-to-itself) than of a self-revelation of the Absolute in history. For Hegel the individual manhood of Jesus is not that wherein the Absolute or the *universale* expresses itself; rather, the manhood of Jesus is "the other" or "the finite," which is "overtaken" by the Infinite.

As is well known, Søren Kierkegaard takes a decidedly different position on the matter:[38] he does not characterize the Infinite or the Universal

---

38. On this point see H. Gerdes, *Das Christusbild Sören Kierkegaards: Verglichen mit der Christologie Hegels und Schleiermachers* (Düsseldorf, 1960), 78-89; H. Fischer, *Die Christologie des Paradoxes: Zur Herkunft und Bedeutung des Christusverständnisses Sören Kierkegaards* (Göttingen, 1970), 48-72; W. Kern, "Menschwerdung Gottes im Spannungsfeld der Interpretationen von Hegel und Kierkegaard," in *Wegmarken der Christologie*, ed. A. Ziegenaus (Donauwörth, 1980), 81-126.

as absolute, but, wholly to the contrary, he ascribes this characteristic to the inexhaustible Factum of the individual. In an essay entitled "The Metaphysical Dimension of the Fact," which in my opinion carries many untapped christological implications, Peter Henrici explains how a fact can be a real symbol *(Realsymbol)* of the Absolute by virtue of its unrepeatable uniqueness. He observes,

> A fact is always *a whole* and is always related to the whole. Something cannot be half or imperfectly the case; something either is or is not the case. If it is the case, then all of the preconditions have been completely fulfilled, one after the other. That is why a fact cannot be "exhaustively thought-through" *(aus-denken)*, it can never be contrived or calculated *post factum*. To attempt to do so would be to produce only a *model* of the fact, which remains abstract and thus to a certain degree generally valid, while the fact itself is always ultimately concrete and supremely individual. In its concrete uniqueness ("this and nothing else is the case"), the fact is nevertheless not isolated. The world does not exist as a totality without this single fact, and this single fact exists only within the context of the world-totality. Its being the case does not place it simply on par with everything else that is and was and will be the case; simply through its being the case, it exerts an influence on anything else that seeks to be the case. "A child yanking his blanket from the crib causes Sirius to wobble," and if Cleopatra's nose had been a tiny bit shorter, it would have altered the course of history.[39]

If we can say that a fact that seems ridiculously insignificant is connected to all existing things, then how much more can be said about a fact that the Christian tradition has taken to be the real self-communication of God in history? Nevertheless, the question remains: What is it about this fact, the existence of "Jesus of Nazareth," that tells us it is not just any state of affairs, but is God's own self-revelation?

Because this, which in technical language is called the "metaphysics of the fact" or the "metaphysics of singularity," is founded on the interconnection of individual beings with all other beings, we can say with Balthasar that at the level of consciousness or personhood this interconnection is not only a datum *(gegeben)* but emerges as a task *(aufgegeben)*. A

---

39. P. Henrici, "Die metaphysische Dimension des Faktums," in Henrici, *Aufbrüche christlichen Denkens,* Kriterien 48 (Einsiedeln, 1978), 27-35, 27f.

person is a fact, i.e., a reality, to the extent that he realizes his potential universal self-transcendence. From this perspective, at least in relation to individual human beings, we can posit a direct proportionality between a person's uniqueness (= *concretum*) and his significance (= *universale*). Specifically in relation to Jesus Christ, this analysis implies that if the man Jesus lives within the conditions of world and history the same relationship to his divine Father that, expressed in trinitarian terms, the eternal Logos *is*, then he is the fact who, because of his divine self-transcendence, makes manifest the unity of all being (= meaning).

A Philosophically Elaborated Concept of Ultimate Meaning and of Jesus Whom the Evangelists Testify Is the Christ

While Hans Urs von Balthasar bases his reflections on a general phenomenology of the gestalt and uses this phenomenology to explain the question of the possibility of coming to know the "figure of glory" *(Herrlichkeitsgestalt),* Hansjürgen Verweyen approaches the problem of the knowability of the Absolute in history by bringing a transcendental-philosophical concept of ultimate meaning into dialogue with the Christ event proclaimed by the Bible.

Verweyen takes his bearings from the early Fichte's thesis that the human being stands as an "I" over against all other human beings who are "not-I," and at the same time can find meaning only by bringing the "not-I" into harmony with the "I."[40] From the perspective of transcendental

---

40. Verweyen sketches the following three steps:
"1) The 'I posits itself' (Fichte), freedom in the strict sense actualizes itself in complete independence from any other and is therefore pure *unity,* unadulterated by any otherness. We can bring this point to evidence by means of the second Cartesian meditation.
"2) Nevertheless: whenever and wherever the I posits itself, it posits itself in *difference.* (The commonsensical thinking of those unpracticed in transcendental reflection may be helped, with some caution, to a grasp of this proposition by the following illustration: The empirical I, who has been alienated from himself through fatigue, can return to himself in this act of self-positing by leaning on something else.) Difference, too, (and for this insight we must unfortunately once again lift ourselves out of our empirical complacency) is ascribed to the I, but not from outside. It is no more possible for the other to implant in me the concept of *otherness* or *difference* than it is for the other to commu-

logic, the difference between the "I" and the "not-I" is rooted in a prereflexive self-assurance possessed by the I, which makes it a unity "capable of difference," i.e., a unity that, concretely speaking, enables the I to do justice to the otherness of the not-I both in its knowing (theoretically) and its doing (practically). For unless there existed a unity capable of difference, the not-I could not even be recognized as the other standing over against the I. Nevertheless, this unity capable of difference is the opposite of Hegel's unity of the Absolute Spirit. According to Verweyen's interpretation of Fichte, the I is forever incapable of "overtaking" *(einholen)* the difference between the I and the not-I. In this respect it is like Sisyphus of Greek mythology, who must tirelessly and repeatedly roll a great stone to the peak of a towering mountain without ever being able to reach the top. Verweyen, in this context, recalls the literary image offered by Camus and Dostoyevsky. May it not be the case, he asks, that the human being is an absurd "I" protesting, for example, against the reality of a tortured child, even though his protest constitutes a part of the very reality against which he is rebelling. How are we to understand this rebellion against a world constituted in such a way that a part of itself, the "I" in revolt, seeks — in vain of course — to distinguish itself and distance itself from this world as the "not-I"?

Only if there exists such a thing as a unity capable of difference can we get beyond this meaninglessness or absurdity. But how, Verweyen asks, can we understand a unity that does not eliminate *(aufhebt)* the difference between the I and the not-I, but instead enables it? He draws his answer from the image ontology of the late Fichte, more specifically, from the observa-

---

nicate my original self-assurance *to me.* To perceive the other *as* other is possible only by virtue of the original unity of the 'I think,' or of free reason. 'Différe(a)nce' — whether spelled with an 'e' or an 'a' — does not function as a fundamental concept for reason in general. This term, however, *does* appropriately characterize reason's fundamental 'thrownness.' For, in fact, it describes the inalterable fate of the I that posits itself independently of any other, insofar as, whenever it posits itself, it finds itself in difference, that is, it posits in a positive or negative relationship to an other.

"3) This already implies that the I emerges as self-contradictory in its innermost structure. The original, absolute unity of my I, which is not mediated to me by any other, forces me into the opposition of difference, which I am unable to evade by my self-positing."

Verweyen, "Gibt es einen philosophisch stringenten Begriff von Inkarnation?" in *Incarnation*, ed. M. M. Olivetti (Padova, 1999), 481-89, here 484f.

tion that absolute unity in purely transcendental-logical difference is possible only if the other that stands over against Absolute Being (i.e., Absolute Unity) is freedom or person, and if at the same time this other commits itself to being nothing but an image of Absolute Being (Absolute Unity).

On the basis of this transcendental-logical concept of absolute unity in difference, Verweyen gives an affirmative answer to the question whether Absolute Being (God) can communicate himself in that which is other (in the finite, in the world, and in history). What these reflections imply for the biblical testimony concerning the Christ event is that Jesus must be capable of being image of the Father (of the Unconditioned Absolute) in precisely the way claimed in the Christian trinitarian doctrine of the eternal Logos or the Son. And in order for Christ (the self-communication of Absolute Being or Absolute Unity) to be able to be all in all, two further steps must be taken: first, "all I's must be transformed into image in relation to each other through definitive decisions,"[41] and second, the space in which the I's encounter one another must become the medium of this reciprocal process of becoming image. As Verweyen explains, "The I becomes an authentic I only if it holds ready within itself a flesh in which all the others that encounter him can come to expression."[42] He then draws a distinction between the horizontal and vertical incarnation of God, and observes that only with the "horizontal incarnation" can God communicate himself in such a way that he, as Absolute Unity, reveals himself in difference.

Furthermore, according to Verweyen, the body is not an obstacle to the ever greater recognition of the other as other, but to the contrary is precisely what makes it possible. This affirmation corresponds to the notion Irenaeus formulated in his criticism of the Gnostics,[43] namely, that man is, or can become, an image of God not by his reason but through his bodily bonds to those other than himself. At the source of this notion lies the conviction that man remains in isolation when he thinks, and that doing so he subordinates what is other than himself to his own thoughts. Allowing oneself to be determined by an other, and ultimately by God himself, is possible only to the extent that — to use Irenaeus's image — man

41. Verweyen, "Gibt es einen philosophisch stringenten Begriff von Inkarnation?" 486.
42. Verweyen, "Gibt es einen philosophisch stringenten Begriff von Inkarnation?" 486.
43. Cf. Irenaeus, *Adversus haereses* 4.pref.4.

exposes himself like moist clay to the hands of the divine potter by entering with his knowing and willing into the flesh. To put it concretely: as long as I just think about my neighbor, I can love him without any effort, because I subordinate him to my own abstractions. The moment I look at him, however, the moment I expose myself bodily to his otherness, share what is my own with him, and thus incarnate my love, then I, more than anyone else, am the one who is most "changed." Verweyen speaks in this context of the "most radical iconoclasm" imaginable, of a Sisyphus who has "grasped his curse as a call." This iconoclasm becomes real when "in my resolution to become image, I first of all unreservedly commit myself to the fact that the other human being is himself free to express himself in infinitely various forms, and, second of all, when the other person is able to recognize precisely this as my unbending resolution in every act I perform."[44]

In the third edition of his work on fundamental theology, Verweyen delves even more explicitly than before into the phenomenon of the corporeality of the subject, drawing in particular on Emmanuel Levinas. As he puts it,

> I interpret the concept "sensuality" *(Sinnlichkeit)* in connection with the transcendental meaning E. Levinas (in his dialogue with E. Husserl) gives it.[45] The concept concerns, as it were, an "intentionality of the sub-

44. Verweyen, *Gottes letztes Wort,* 173.

45. "As Levinas understands it, the subjectivity that lies outside of the difference between being and nothing has to be conceived in terms of a passivity that eludes the I insofar as it posits itself as itself. In self-reflection, the I grasps a self, which it recognizes as identical to itself and by which mediates to itself the identity of self-consciousness. But this means that it can never get behind itself in reflection and therefore can never ground itself in itself. This incapacity of the I is nevertheless nothing but a statement of what *cannot* be said about subjectivity, which does not yet say anything about what it is. In his early writings, Levinas developed the I's bondage to itself as the burden-character of Being, and conceived the other as what allows the I to be freed from its self-bondage through transcendence. In the later phase of his thinking, Levinas focuses his attention on the subject himself and on the possibility of viewing the self as dependent on otherness, a possibility given by the self's character of inescapability, which results from the I's inability to correspond perfectly to itself. On this side of being and self-consciousness, subjectivity emerges into view, not as a striving to free oneself from self-bondage, but as the inevitable bearing of the burden of Being and the universe, to which the other calls the self and by virtue of which the subject receives its justification. On this basis, Levinas does not interpret the subject as substantiality, existing in itself, but rather in terms of the original meaning of the very word 'subject,' a meaning that im-

ject that precedes all subjective intentionalities." Levinas (correctly) refuses to accept as adequate and original any understanding of the subject that presumes I am able to encounter what is other only in the screen of my projected categories, whether they be *a priori* or *a posteriori*. On the contrary, by virtue of my senses, I am always already involved consciously or unconsciously with what is other, who has not yet been "caught in the net of my categories," or, to put it another way, the other has always already entered into me in a primordial way.[46]

With Levinas, Verweyen affirms that in the encounter with the face of the other, the unconditional ought becomes immediately evident. Insofar as the question concerning the origin of this unconditional ought remains unanswered, however, the demand to do unconditional justice to the other acquires a certain arbitrariness. In other words, what is at issue is the question: Doesn't this exposing oneself to the other lead to the annihilation of self? What grounds are there to expose oneself to the other? What is the reason for the toilsome path of the aforementioned iconoclasm? Why can't we instead view everything other (all difference) in a Buddhistic sense as mere appearance? What keeps me from striving after total annihilation in nirvana as my ultimate goal?

In the new edition of his main work, Verweyen answers this question in the following way: an answer to the problem of the chasm that we ourselves are unable to close between formal unconditionality and the material conditionality of our freedom, between the demand to do perfect justice to the otherness of the other and the inevitably imperfect realization of this task in any given instance is "indeed possible only given the assumption that, in the end, an Incarnation of the Absolute itself emerges to help the constantly frustrated efforts[47] of freedom to incarnate itself as an

---

plies passivity: subjectivity is the event of subjection *(subjéction)*, being 'thrown under' the other." U. Dickmann, *Subjektivität als Verantwortung: Die Ambivalenz des Humanum bei Emmanuel Levinas und ihre Bedeutung für die theologische Anthropologie*, Tübinger Studien zur Theologie und Philosophie 16 (Tübingen and Basel, 1999), 373f.

46. Verweyen, *Gottes letztes Wort* (Regensburg, 2000), 168 n. 44.

47. "The realm of otherness, to which freedom refers, in order just to be able to be *there* at all, does not *allow* itself to be understood exhaustively as a potential medium for interpersonal recognition. It does not matter how resolutely an individual persists in his commitment to forge his body into an image of an other individual: As he approaches death, his body and the sense-world slip away from his control. His will, though it remains 'moist' for sculpting, cannot prevent his body from drying out more and more, from hardening and

image of the Absolute."[48] This vertical incarnation would be realized in a human being able to make the whole of his human nature an image of the unconditional recognition of the otherness of the other, which according to Christian belief the inner-trinitarian Son *is* in his recognition of the Father.

The four Evangelists present Jesus each in his own way as the one who does not perish in the exposure of himself unconditionally to the otherness of the other; instead, he is the one who reveals himself as the Christ — the way, the truth, and the life for all human beings of all times.[49] In con-

---

becoming inflexible, all the way to the biological structures and physiological processes that are most fundamental for free and reasonable activity." Verweyen, *Gottes letztes Wort,* 184.

48. Verweyen, *Gottes letztes Wort,* 184.

49. "J. G. Fichte was the first to show, in the proof of the interpersonal constitution of self-consciousness that he undertakes in §§1-3 of his 'Foundation of Natural Right' (1796), what was unthinkable for Lessing and Kant: how an autonomous freedom can be awakened to unconditional moral obligation through historical events. . . . Even the most primitive effort — for example, the desire to gain possession of something through force — is the expression of an I that wants to posit itself unconditionally in the 'not-I' (an I that of course in this case does not yet have a hold on the conditions of possibility of this self-positing and therefore of its own essence). In order to attain to its true essence, and in this respect to *'conscience'* (consciousness, self-consciousness, and moral conscience), the I has need of a determinate act of another subject, which Fichte calls a 'summons' *(Aufforderung).* In this fundamental interpersonal event, the experience of the *real ought* is grounded: despite the unsurmountable difference in which I posit all of my acts, I desire to be identical. I am aided in this through the image of my freedom that the other presents to me by recognizing me as a free I (for example in the mother's smile). The other who recognizes me affirms me, but not only (and at least not primarily) as a function of the other's freedom, which must be responded to in its formal unconditionality. The other desires that I truly attain to a genuine human existence, rich with content, and therefore in the image that he presents to me of my freedom, he presents at the same time an image of that which he takes to be necessary for a full human existence (Fichte speaks of the act of summons, which constitutes self-consciousness, as the beginning of education). Insofar as I will *myself* in the image of the *other,* I affirm at the same time the determinate understanding of freedom that the other projects, which is mediated in that image, as integral to *my* freedom. This is what constitutes the phenomenon of obligation: the recognition of an understanding of freedom, which I have not myself determined, as the goal of my most intimate freedom. Insofar as we are dealing with an other who truly concerns himself with *me* as a being that must be respected in its integrity (and foreignness), and at the same time we are dealing with the fact that I allow the freedom that is determined by the other to lay a claim on me, a freedom that also penetrates the other *as a call that places an unconditional call on himself,* what we have before us is what was characterized in the foregoing phenomenological description as a *witness.* The other enables me to actualize myself as identity in difference, insofar as he summons me

crete terms this means that everyone who confesses Jesus as the Christ, not as a matter of convention but as a matter of conviction, "must experience in the depth of his being that he himself is recognized as an image of God. Doing so, he is compelled to perceive the unconditional demand and the firm hope to discover all human beings as images of God, so that through the reciprocal recognition of infinitely many images, the very Image of the Absolute himself finally comes to expression."[50]

The Evangelists bear witness to this. Those who nailed Jesus of Nazareth to the cross did not have the last word; instead it goes to the one who acknowledged them unconditionally even as they flogged him. Verweyen refuses to interpret the centurion's confession under the cross — "Truly, this was the Son of God!" — as a post-Easter superimposition. Mark the theologian, he writes, puts this confession in the mouth of the pagan centurion because it was already *possible* before Easter, and especially under the cross, to recognize Jesus as the one whose recognition of the otherness of the other, whose transformation into the image of the Absolute, was not a defeat but a victory, not a loss of self but a gaining of self through total self-gift. In opposition to Thomas Pröpper,[51] Verweyen[52] wholeheartedly affirms that the one human being who *is* the relationship of the inner-trinitarian Son to the Father within the conditions of world and history is able to turn his body — or allow it to be turned — into such a clear image

as a free being to that which represents for him a human obligation, and which he therefore passes on to me. Historical events are indispensable not only as acts of general interpersonal recognition for the actualization of my autonomy. The original actualization of my self as real and not only supposed freedom more specifically constitutes itself in the act of bearing witness. . . . Witness is . . . the genuine locus for the knowledge and transmission of an event that lays claim to moral reason. It makes a 'past event' present . . . insofar as the witness allows a claim to be laid on him in a twofold sense; on the one hand, in relation to the one on whose behalf he is called to bear witness, and, on the other hand, in relation to the one whom the call is intended to reach." Verweyen, *Botschaft eines Toten?* 129-31.

50. Verweyen, *Botschaft eines Toten?* 194.

51. Cf. T. Pröpper, *Erlösungsglaube und Freiheitsgeschichte: Eine Skizze zur Soteriologie,* 3rd ed. (Munich, 1991), esp., 246ff.; Pröpper, "Erstphilosophischer Begriff oder Aufweis letztgültigen Sinnes? Anfragen an Hansjürgen Verweyens 'Grundriß der Fundamentaltheologie,'" *Theologische Quartalschrift* 174 (1994): 272-87; Pröpper, "Sollensevidenz, Sinnvollzug und Offenbarung: Im Gespräch mit Hansjürgen Verweyen," in *Hoffnung, die Gründe nennt: Zu Hansjürgen Verweyens Projekt einer erstphilosophischen Glaubensverantwortung,* ed. G. Larcher, K. Müller, and T. Pröpper (Regensburg, 1996), 27-48.

52. Cf. H. Verweyen, "Glaubensverantwortung heute: Zu den 'Anfragen' von Thomas Pröpper," *Theologische Quartalschrift* 174 (1994): 288-303.

of the Unconditional precisely *in* the crucified recognition of the otherness of the other, that even where the violent hatred of the executioner seems to triumph, he shows himself to be the one whom God has not abandoned. In trinitarian terms he shows himself to be the Son who is borne by the Father even in physical death.

Behind this difference between Pröpper and Verweyen lies a difference between two different philosophical premises. In Verweyen's image ontology, inspired by the late Fichte, there is the image that is image *(Abbild)* (and therefore different from that which it images [*Urbild*]), precisely to the extent that it is one with that which it images. In christological terms: the more the man Jesus realizes his humanity (an image of God who is the trinitarian recognition of the other as other), the more clearly he reveals his Sonship, as the one who is the unconditional image of the eternal Father. By contrast Pröpper appeals to what Hermann Krings described as the unresolvable antinomy between formal unconditionality and the material conditionality of human freedom. Man's commitment to his own freedom is formally unconditional; man's "I," because it is endowed with freedom, can relate itself in principle to every other (every not-I). And nevertheless, the realization of this formally unconditional freedom is necessarily bound to a limited, finite, and concrete content. In other words, the concrete actualization can never recapitulate the formal unconditionality of freedom.

With respect to Jesus Christ, this antinomy implies that since he is the incarnate love of the eternal Logos, he can indeed relate himself unconditionally to the Thou of the other; he can love the other unconditionally. However, he cannot adequately manifest the unconditionality of his love through the finite acts of his human nature. There remains an unbridgeable chasm between formal unconditionality and material conditionality. In light of Krings's analysis of freedom, Pröpper considers it impossible that the earthly Jesus could have been unambiguously recognizable as the Christ, as the Absolute in history. Though he characterizes his historically perceivable acts of love as a *Realsymbol* of his true divinity, Pröpper strictly excludes the possibility that a *Realsymbol* can eliminate the aforementioned chasm between the unconditionality of the one who expresses himself and the conditionality of the expression.

In my opinion the debate between Verweyen and Pröpper over the question concerning the knowability of the uniqueness of Christ recalls the almost forgotten dialogue between Joseph Ratzinger and Walter

Karl-Heinz Menke

Kasper. Reacting to Ratzinger's *Introduction to Christianity*, which had just appeared, Kasper objected to what he saw as an idealistic identification of freedom and necessity, history and reason, and faith and love;[53] his reservations were especially prompted by the passage in which Ratzinger seeks to bridge the gap Lessing described between the Jesus of history and the Christ of faith by claiming that the love of the historical Jesus was manifest as the divine identity between being and act. Indeed, Ratzinger draws a distinction between Bultmann's inauthentic actualism and the more radical actualism of the figure of Jesus presented by the Bible.[54] While Bultmann takes for granted that the Lordship or divine Sonship of the Redeemer became actual event *(Akt)* only in the existence of individual believers, the New Testament, Ratzinger argues, insists that Jesus' being can-

53. "The theological implication of the synthesis of reason and history is the identification of faith and love. . . . The coincidence of faith and love, as Ratzinger characterizes it, indeed, the assertion that 'love is faith' ([*Introduction to Christianity*], 167) has to be thought through logically to the end . . . as leading to secularization and to the 'coincidence of adoration and brotherly love' (206); this ultimately makes faith into a merely ideological and salvation-historical superstructure erected on top of conviviality, even if this is the opposite of what Ratzinger explicitly intends (237). The latent idealism and secularism in Ratzinger's *Introduction* is ultimately due to his platonizing point of departure, because of which the properly Christian scandal of the '*Logos sarx egeneto*' (Jn 1:14) constantly falls under the mastery and the law-boundedness of Greek philosophy's concept of reality, contrary to the constantly protested good intentions of the author and despite his consistent emphasis of the positivity of Christianity (30ff., 62f., 153f., 199ff., 219f., 267f.). The subsequent idealistic synthesis of reason and history allows us to interpret Ratzinger at one time existentially, and at another time historically-bodily, with the same indecisiveness and ambivalence that plagues Hegel. In a certain sense, he thus places himself outside of possible attack, since he is able to counter any contradiction of one position by adopting the other. But this simply eliminates the very positivity of Christianity he had previously argued for." W. Kasper, "Das Wesen des Christlichen," *Theologische Revue* 65 (1969): 182-88, here 185.

54. In the form of actualism that Bultmann defends, "the actual *being* of the man Jesus remains static behind the event of divinity and lordship as the being of any randomly chosen man, who remains ultimately untouched by this event and is only the accidental place where the event catches fire, the place where the ever-actual encounter with God himself becomes a reality for whomever hears the word. And just as the being of Jesus remains static behind the event, the being of the individual can also be touched by the divine always only in the zone of the 'ever actual' event. Here, too, the encounter with God occurs only in the split-second instant of the event, and being remains outside of its reach. In my opinion, in such a theology we see a sort of despair of the existing man who does not allow himself to hope that Being itself could ever come to act." J. Ratzinger, *Einführung in das Christentum: Vorlesungen über das Apostolische Glaubensbekenntnis* (Munich, 1968), 183f.

not be separated from his activity, nor his person from his work. As Ratzinger puts it, "His being is pure *actualitas* of 'from' and 'for.' It is precisely *because* his being can no longer be separated from his *actualitas* that he is identical with God."[55] Kasper does not object to Ratzinger's critique of Bultmann, but rather to the inferences he draws from it. According to Kasper, Jesus does not reveal himself as the Christ through a prior identification of being and act, history and meaning. In the beginning there is only the historical fact; historians may not be able to excavate the precise character of this fact, but they may nevertheless purify it of the debris of presumptive interpretations. And the contingency of this fact cannot be done away with by defining Jesus Platonically as the incarnation of the "love principle" or as the "paradigmatic human being." Instead, from the very beginning the recognition of the historical Jesus as the Christ is a matter of faith; and only the eyes of this faith can see that God has revealed himself (as unconditional love) in this particular man, Jesus.[56]

Verweyen adopts Ratzinger's approach without, like he does, rooting the revelation of divine love in the identification of act and being. Instead, his image ontology takes the difference between the historical Jesus and the eternal Logos as seriously as it does their unity: difference and unity between image and that which is imaged grow in direct proportion to each other. Verweyen in no way denies that Jesus Christ, as true man, lives his relationship with the Father, which is identical with the person of the eternal Son, within the conditions of finitude — or, as Krings puts it, under the conditions of the antinomy between the formal unconditionality and

55. Ratzinger, *Einführung in das Christentum*, 184.

56. "Within the horizon of historical thinking, even the unique and unrepeatable significance of the earthly Jesus and his fate can be more clearly grounded. Jesus Christ is, from this perspective, only an *exemplum* of man, but at the same time the unique and enduring basis that first opens and makes possible for us in faith what God intended humanity to be. The historical inquiry into the earthly (historical) Jesus is thereby turned into an immanent element of theology, and it becomes impossible to dismiss it as a caricature. The essence of Christianity no longer allows itself to be described as the 'love principle,' but rather to be determined by the phrase 'God is love' (1 Jn 4:8). This phrase does not express a principle, but is rather the reflection on the event in which God revealed himself as love in Jesus Christ; only because we have experienced this in faith can we therefore say ourselves that God is the love he reveals himself to be. This is why faith is in a certain sense prior to love. By contrast, Ratzinger stands the biblical and traditional understanding of the relationship between faith and love (DS 1578) precisely on its head, and his position takes on clear contours and a contradictory character when viewed next to the Christian faith." Kasper, 186 n. 53.

material conditionality of his freedom. But with Balthasar he takes for granted that it is precisely the unrepeatable fact of the uniqueness of an individual human being that can reveal the interconnection of all beings (the meaning of all being). With Balthasar and Ratzinger he sees in the self-surrender of the crucified one the absolutely decisive place of the self-revelation of the unconditional in the conditional.

The affirmation, which Balthasar, Ratzinger, and Verweyen all make to the same extent, namely, that the self-revelation of the Absolute in history is not only possible but also knowable, cannot fail to have implications for our very image of God. If God has expressed his very self in the historical fact of Jesus of Nazareth, then we are no longer permitted to look for his omnipotence beyond the cross; then his omnipotence has become visible precisely *on* the cross; then this omnipotence is not something completely different from the crucified love of Jesus, but is identical with it; then Easter faith means that the apparently (!) impotent love of the crucified one is stronger than the power of the mighty, stronger than all the power of evil.

At Easter we celebrate the fact that the defenseless love of the trinitarian God was stronger than the crucifying hatred of the executioner. This superabundant strength did not occur *after* Good Friday, but *on* Good Friday. God does not show himself *first* as crucified love and *afterward* as the omnipotence that triumphs with a victorious gesture. No, God is omnipotent *as* crucified love, and *only as* crucified love. If the omnipotence we sing about on Easter were to mean that God could have prevented any Good Friday had he so desired, then Jesus would not have been the *self-revelation* of God; and then, to put it bluntly, we would be celebrating a cynic who failed to prevent his Son's *via crucis* when he could have. No, even if we celebrate Easter two days after Good Friday, the revelation of God's omnipotence may not be separated from the event of the cross. Easter means that Jesus was completely and utterly the Son, that he was able to allow the Father's will or Torah to penetrate so deeply into his anxiety, his suffering, and his death that he "comprehended" (Balthasar) the cross that seemed to triumph over him. Or to put it another way: physical death did not destroy Jesus because even in physical death his relationship to the Father (and thus to the life that cannot die) remained unbroken. For us this means that whoever "allows Jesus Christ to penetrate" into his questioning and seeking, struggles and battles, suffering and dying, whether consciously or unconsciously, to him the Holy Scriptures promise the experience of a power that — even if it cannot force anything (and thus appears from outside to be "impotent") — nevertheless proves to be stronger than any cross or any experience of meaninglessness.